The Patchwork Quilt Design & Coloring Book

by Judith LaBelle Larsen and
Carol Waugh Gull

Butterick Publishing

We dedicate this book to

Anna Nelson Larsen
J. L. L.

We would like to thank Robert Driscoll for his help in setting up the charts in this book and Betty Ferguson for helping us in our research of the quilt patterns.

Library of Congress Catalog Card Number: 76-057296
International Standard Book Number: 0-88421-028-6

Copyright © 1977 by Butterick Publishing
708 Third Avenue, New York, New York 10017
A Division of American Can Company

Color Illustrations by Judy Larsen, Carol Gull, and Marilyn Gong
Illustrations by Phoebe Gaughan
Book Design by Betty Binns
Cover Design by Sallie Baldwin
PRINTED IN U.S.A.

Second Printing, July 78

Contents

Project Plan for Using a Traditional Design

1 Decide:

- the size of your finished quilt—twin, full, queen, king
- which of the 50 traditional designs you will use
- the size block you will construct

2 Turn to the page with the design you have chosen. Use the chart that corresponds to your block size and look at the following information:

- template code
- total number of pieces of each shape needed for the size of your finished quilt

3 Use the yardage charts beginning on page 215 to determine the yardage requirements for each shape.

4 Buy fabric and prepare it for cutting.

5 Use the template codes and the template outlines to make all the templates required for your design.

6 Use the templates to cut out the number of pieces needed of each shape.

7 Construct the blocks.

8 Set into the quilt top.

9 Quilt and finish.

Project Plan for an Original Design

1 Design your block and quilt top using any grid in this book. (Any of the 100 color variations in Chapter 3 may be used as a starting point for a design.)

2 Use the Designer's Worksheet to determine the template code and the total number of pieces needed for the size of your finished quilt. (Designer's Worksheet begins on page 193.)

3 Use the yardage charts beginning on page 215 to determine the yardage requirements for each shape.

Steps 4, 5, 6, 7, 8, 9 same as for Traditional Design.

How to Use
This Book

Designing and making a patchwork quilt is great fun and a satisfying experience. Unless, of course, you miscalculate and buy only half the fabric you need. Or you choose the design by looking at one block and then dislike the overall design which results when several blocks are sewn together to form the quilt top. Or you finish the quilt only to discover that it doesn't fit your bed.

The Patchwork Quilt Design and Coloring Book was written to help beginner and expert alike to avoid these and other common pitfalls of making a patchwork quilt. But this book does more than help you avoid mistakes and problems. It is full of information which takes the drudgery out of quilt making and puts the fun and creativity back in.

The book has a workbook format. There are pattern outlines on which you can experiment with color and design, fill-in-the-blank worksheets to take you step-by-step through the process of planning your quilt, charts to replace all of the calculations you would otherwise have to do to figure out how much fabric you need. In fact from now on, when you make a quilt, you will know exactly how much fabric to buy, exactly how to construct it, and exactly what it will look like—before your start.

Beginning with the chapter on color, you will learn how to choose colors to suit your taste and decor, how colors interact when several are used together, and why patterned fabric must be chosen with care and its use carefully planned. You will begin to develop an understanding of how the use of several blocks placed side by side can affect the overall design of the quilt top.

Once you understand some basic principles of color and design, the grids in the *50 Traditional Patchwork Designs* chapter will enable you to experiment with the impact of design and color on any or all of the fifty basic designs outlined. On these pages, you will see the traditional configuration of the block along with two alternative configurations which indicate the endless design possibilities inherent in each design. Complete yardage and template charts are also provided so that you can make any of the traditional designs for any standard-size bed (twin, full, queen, and king).

If you aren't satisfied with a design from one of the traditional grids, you can achieve a very different effect by separating the blocks with lattice or by rotating every other block, and we have provided grids to illustrate each of these alternatives. Or you may want to try a pattern from the *Overall Design* chapter, where each quilt top is composed of only one or two templates and the design is not based on individual blocks, but rather is a single entity which covers the quilt top.

Hopefully, after trying out all of these alternatives, you will be able to pick a favorite design. The next step is *Putting It All Together.* In this chapter, you will learn how to determine the finished size of your quilt top, how to plan borders, and how to select the right fabric and prepare it for cutting. You'll also find tips on machine sewing and block construction. And, of course, you'll learn how to assemble the finished blocks to form your quilt top. Guidance is also given on quilting by machine and by hand, quilting by the block, and tieing.

If you have chosen a traditional design that is illustrated in this book, you can use the charts in the *Yardage Charts* chapter to determine the exact amount of fabric you need to buy for your quilt top. However, if you've designed your own, there is an easy *Designer's Worksheet* to show you how to determine the number, size, and shape of the templates in your design. From that information, you can quickly refer to the *Yardage Charts* to determine your fabric needs.

The *Templates* chapter includes traceable outlines of most of the templates you will need to make any design in this book. Also, complete instructions are given for making your own templates from scratch.

If you are anything like us, once you begin to experiment with color, fabric, and shapes, you will have a difficult time deciding which design you like best. But what an enjoyable problem to ponder! So get out your colored pencils, open up your mind, and start designing! It's easy and fun and, who knows, maybe you'll finally develop just the right design and make that quilt you've been talking about for years.

1
Color and Design

Many of the traditional patchwork designs presented in this book are probably familiar to you. Handed down from generation to generation, these patchwork patterns have been in wide and common use.

Perhaps the major reason for their popularity is the limitless variety which the form allows. No two quilts using the same basic pattern are exactly alike. While the difference between them may lie in the size of the blocks used or in the type of border, it is far more likely that the uniqueness of any quilt will result from the quiltmaker's choice and arrangement of colors.

Colors old and new

There is a much wider range of colored fabric available to you than the frontier woman ever imagined possible. We expect that you will want to make use of all the colors available now and therefore we choose not to limit the colors used in the illustrations to those colors which were available in fabrics one hundred years ago.

Further, the colors which you see in most old quilts are far from the colors in which the quilts were originally made. Both age and wear have faded the original colors. Fading—and sometimes even the rotting of the material—also has resulted because the chemicals and techniques used in the early dyeing processes were not so sophisticated as those in use today.

If, however, you want your new quilt to have the look of a faded antique quilt, you may want to try bleaching the material slightly before you begin to work with it, to dull the colors a bit. Or you may want to buy old, second-hand clothes made of fabrics which are still sturdy and use that fabric for your patches. See page 32.

Choosing the colors for your quilt

Since you will be investing a good deal of time and money in your quilt, it makes good sense to choose colors that you will enjoy working with and having around you.

If the last time you seriously thought about color choice was for a grammar school essay or art project, it will be worth your while to give the topic some consideration now. Your taste may have changed and so have the colors in which fabrics are available.

Look with fresh eyes at the things with which you have surrounded yourself. Which area of your home is most pleasing to you and what role do the colors of the decor play in making you respond positively? What colors are your favorite articles of clothing and what color accessories do you feel comfortable wearing with them?

What scenes in nature and what objects of art do you most appreciate? Pay close attention to the colors that predominate and the flashes of accent color. The accents are often the factor which distinguish an ordinary scene from a memorable one.

Many craftspeople keep a notebook or file containing examples of the colors and color combinations they find most pleasing. Such a file makes an excellent reference source. Having many ideas readily at hand is useful when you begin a new craft project and want to get your creative juices flowing. Magazine advertisements and pictures from decorating or fashion magazines make an excellent source of color ideas and are easily clipped and saved. Postcard reproductions of fine-art masterpieces are another fertile source of ideas.

When choosing the colors for your quilt top, you should also consider the setting in which the quilt will be used. Your quilt will be an original work of art that could easily be the focus of attention in any room. Thus, you will want to be sure that the quilt color and design coordinate, rather than clash, with the decor of the room where the quilt will be used.

THE COLOR WHEEL

A tool which may be very useful to you in developing a greater understanding of color and the relationships between colors is the color wheel (*Illustration 1*).

The basic color wheel contains red, yellow, and blue. These primary colors form the basis of the analysis of color which follows. All other colors are created by mixing two of these colors in varying proportions. These primary colors themselves are pure—they do not contain any other color. Blue, for example, contains no yellow or red.

Illustration 1
The Color Wheel

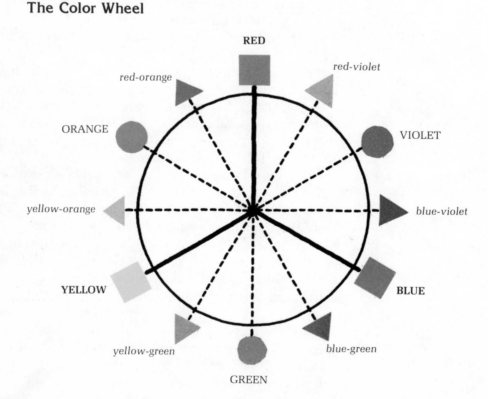

The colors which are obtained by mixing two adjacent primary colors in equal proportions are the secondary colors, represented by the circles on the color wheel. The secondary colors are orange, green, and violet.

The triangles in our color wheel represent the tertiary colors—the colors which result from combining a primary color and one of its secondary colors. For example, red and orange combine to form red-orange.

As you no doubt suspect by now, this mixing of adjacent colors can go on and on to create an infinite range of colors. However, for our purposes, the twelve colors presented will suffice.

Colors which are opposite each other on the color wheel are termed "complementary" colors. If they are used together each makes the other appear more intense. Note how clean and clear the red and green each appear in this **Shoo-fly** block (*Illustration 2*).

An "analogous" color scheme is created when two or more adjacent colors are used together. In the **Anvil** block below we have used shades of red-violet, violet, and blue-violet. Adjacent colors which lie between two primary colors work well together and form pleasing color schemes because each is created from a mixture of the same two primary colors (*Illustration 3*).

RIGHT:
Illustration 2
Shoofly

FAR RIGHT:
Illustration 3
Anvil

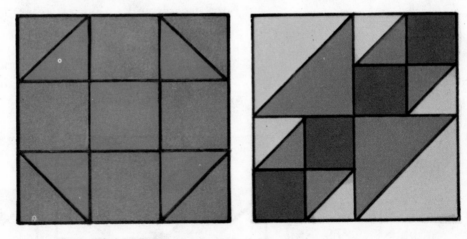

Colors working together

In your consideration of the colors that please you, you will notice that how any color appears to you and how you respond to it depends to a great extent upon the other colors that are used with it.

To facilitate your study of color, we will explore some of these properties of colors working together.

WARM AND COOL COLORS

You have probably heard colors referred to as either "warm" or "cool". We speak in these terms because the colors actually appear to have different temperatures. Reds, oranges, and yellows appear warm. Greens, blues, and violets appear cool. For example, the blue **Barbara Frietchie Star** (*Illustration 4*) appears much cooler than the pink star (*Illustration 5*).

RIGHT:
Illustration 4
Barbara Frietchie Star

FAR RIGHT:
Illustration 5
Barbara Frietchie Star

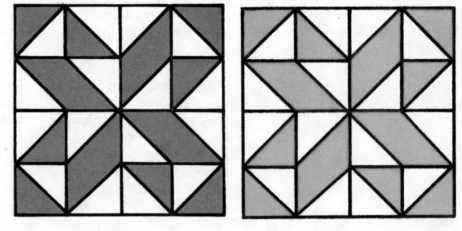

When a warm and a cool color are mixed, the apparent temperature of the resulting color will depend on the proportion of each and on which color predominates. For example, the two violet colors (*Illustrations 6 and 7*) are both the result of a combination of blue (a cool color) and red (a warm color). Notice that in the violet in Illustration 6, blue predominates and the color appears cooler than the violet in Illustration 7, in which red predominates.

RIGHT:
Illustration 6
Barbara Frietchie Star

FAR RIGHT:
Illustration 7
Barbara Frietchie Star

Color temperatures interact when colors are used together. A color scheme that is predominantly red can be cooled by incorporating blue into the design, or its warmth can be heightened by using yellow. The same red was used for both stars, yet note how much more vibrant and hot the star in Illustration 8 appears compared to the one in Illustration 9.

When warm and cool colors are used together, the warm colors advance and the cool colors recede. Look again at the red star on the blue background. Notice how the star seems to stand apart from the background. When the red star is on the yellow background, however, both seem to remain on the same plane.

RIGHT:
Illustration 8
Barbara Frietchie Star

FAR RIGHT:
Illustration 9
Barbara Frietchie Star

CONTRASTING VALUES

Each color has a wide range of possible "values" or intensities: it may range in shade from very light to very dark. The values of brown, for instance, may range from the very palest to the very darkest brown. The monochromatic color scheme created by using several values of the same color may be very pleasing, as in the **Brown Goose** block (*Illustration 10*).

If the extremes of a color's values are placed next to each other, the contrast will appear to heighten the value of each. The most striking example of this phenomenon is a color scheme that uses black and white. Notice how the white area framed by the thick black border appears whiter than the rest of this page (*Illustration 11*).

Illustration 10
Brown Goose

Illustration 11

The same heightening occurs with any color when very light shades are placed against very dark shades. For example, the variation of **Friendship Star** appears deeper when placed against a dark blue background (*Illustration 12*) than when used against a white background (*Illustration 13*).

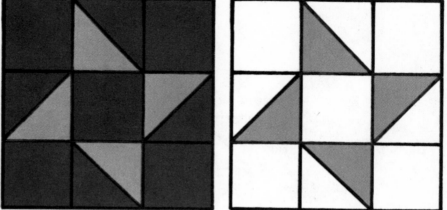

The background color used to create this heightened effect does not, of course, have to be a different shade of the same color used for the pattern motif. The **Old Maid's Puzzle** blocks illustrate that a background of medium value provides less contrast and thus heightens the motif color less than a very light or very dark background (*Illustration 14*).

Notice how the two center squares of white in the block on the right appear much whiter than the same squares in the designs where the background provides less contrast.

Illustration 14
Old Maid's Puzzle

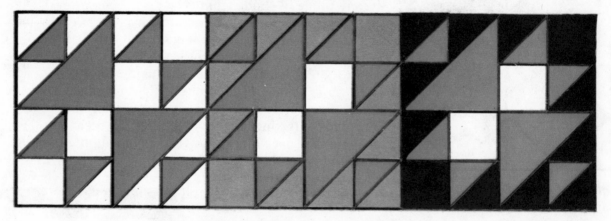

The color of the background against which a color is placed will also influence the three-dimensional quality which the block appears to have. When the primary colors are placed on a white background, the blue advances more than the red, the

Illustration 15
Ribbons

red more than the yellow. Just the opposite occurs when the background is black. Then the yellow advances the most, followed by the red and blue (*Illustration 15*).

The use of certain colors can also make one area of a design appear to have more weight than another area. Dark colors appear to be heavier than light colors. Note this effect in the **Old Maid's Puzzle** blocks (*Illustration 14*). Another example is provided by the **Prairie Queen** blocks (*Illustration 16*). Note the striking increase in the apparent weight of the central motif when it is colored dark green, rather than white.

Illustration 16
Prairie Queen

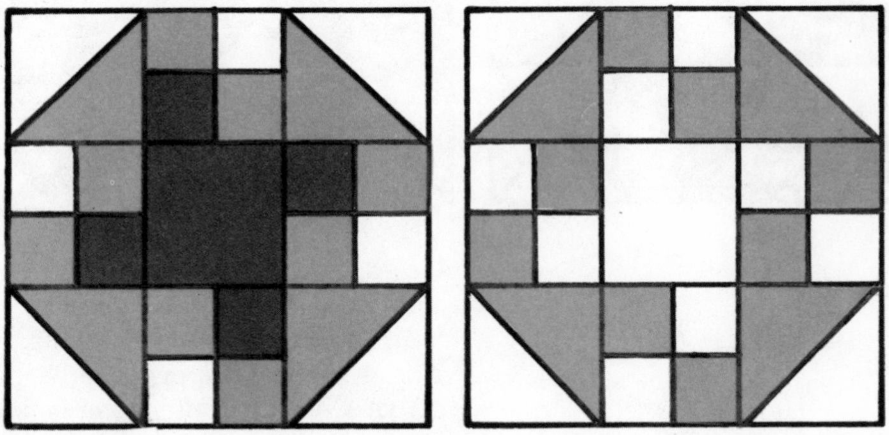

Patchwork design Now that we have explored the basic principles of color use, we will turn our attention to design, the interrelating of color and shape.

The basic block which you choose for your quilt may appear one way when viewed in isolation and quite another once it is "set" with several other blocks. Anticipating this result and learning how to make it work for you is an important part of working with patchwork design.

Illustration 17 **Letter X**

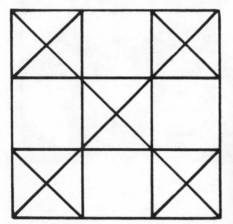

Illustration 17 **Letter X**

Illustration 18 **Letter X**

Let us use **Letter X** as an example. The block outline, the traditional configuration, and a group of four traditional blocks are shown in Illustrations 17, 18, and 19.

Notice how designs appear in the group of blocks that were not apparent in looking at the single block. Parts of hour

Illustration 19 **Letter X**

glasses and interlocking diamonds are only two of the patterns that can be seen when several blocks are set together. Thus, an exciting overall pattern results from a block design which, viewed by itself, appears only mildly interesting.

A very different effect can be achieved by using four colors, rather than two, and changing the placement of color. In Illustration 20, the **Letter X** block has been colored so that it is reminiscent of the traditional appliqué pattern, **Meadow Lily.**

Yet when four of the blocks are set together, the corner "flowers" form pinwheels and the design has more the look of a tile floor than an arrangement of flowers (*Illustration 21*).

The purpose of this section is to help you become more sensitive to the designs block patterns form when set together in groups and to help you learn how to make this design

Illustration 20
Letter X

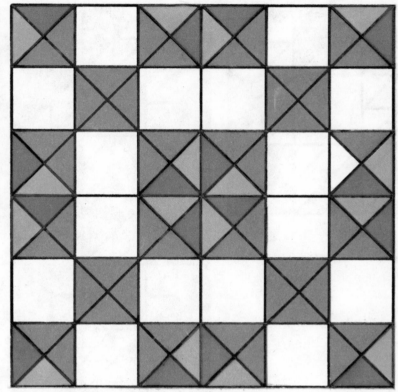

Illustration 21
Letter X

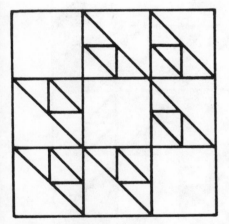

Illustration 22
Cat's Cradle

phenomenon work for you. The grids in this book allow you to see how your choice and placement of color will affect the overall design of your quilt. Otherwise, you might be in for some surprises—and not all of them pleasant—when the quilt is set.

Blocks having diagonal designs are particularly likely to form patterns that extend across the quilt's surface. Let's take **Cat's Cradle** as an example. We begin once again with an outline of the block, the single block in its traditional coloration, and a group of blocks (*Illustrations 22, 23, and 24*). Notice that the placement of the large triangles creates a diagonal movement that extends from block to block.

This effect can be accentuated by the choice and placement of color. In Illustrations 25 and 26, different colors and a different placement of color have been used. Notice that when four blocks are set together, the light, bright diagonals of orange and yellow contrast with the darker brown and green and are much more pronounced than any of the diagonals in the blocks of traditional color—another good example of colors being heightened by contrast, as explained earlier in this chapter.

Illustration 23
Cat's Cradle

Illustration 24
Cat's Cradle

Illustration 25
Cat's Cradle

Illustration 26
Cat's Cradle

A more fanciful sense of movement and design has been created using **Water Wheel.** In Illustration 27, four of the traditional blocks have been set together, forming an intricate and interesting design.

But when we were looking at the grid for this design, we were struck by the resemblance of the pattern formed by the large triangles to the curling stripes on candy canes. This observation suggested the striking design in Illustration 28. Notice that while the large triangles form a pattern running vertically and horizontally across the page, the small squares move diagonally. The use of bold red against the stark white background adds to the liveliness of the design.

All of the designs illustrated thus far have depended upon the coloration of the standard block to form designs which extend across the quilt. But unique designs can be created by looking for patterns which are not contained within the traditional block and which depend upon the combination of several different blocks. Let us go back to the **Letter X** (Illustration 29) for an example. In Illustration 30, six blocks of **Letter X** have been colored to create a design which is entirely different from either the traditional design or our previous examples. The design shown on this grid is not based on a component contained within any individual block.

To explore the full artistic potential offered by patchwork, you must be open to the multitude of designs possible on any given grid. In Illustration 31, one **Texas Star** block has been colored in the lower right corner. The design appears simple and straightforward. The major portion of the grid has been colored with a bold, interesting design which can be produced by repeating a single block. To form this design, every other row is turned upside down when the blocks are joined to make the quilt top. Nevertheless, the design is strikingly different from what one would expect from looking at the one block of the traditional **Texas Star.** The central portion framed by the interconnecting square motifs would be a splendid place for some fancy quilting patterns.

Approach the grids with an open mind and a curious eye. Whether you use a traditional configuration or try to develop an original design, keep in mind the principles of color use which are outlined in the beginning of this chapter. To illustrate further the conjunction of design and color we will use **Dutchman's Puzzle** (*Illustration 32*). The single block on the right side of the grid has been colored in the traditional way, using two primary colors, yellow and blue. Notice how the blue advances from the light background.

Illustration 27
Water Wheel

Illustration 28
Water Wheel

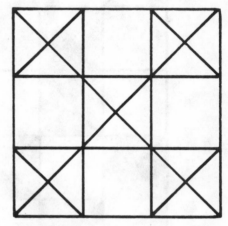

Illustration 29
Letter X

Illustration 30 **Letter X**

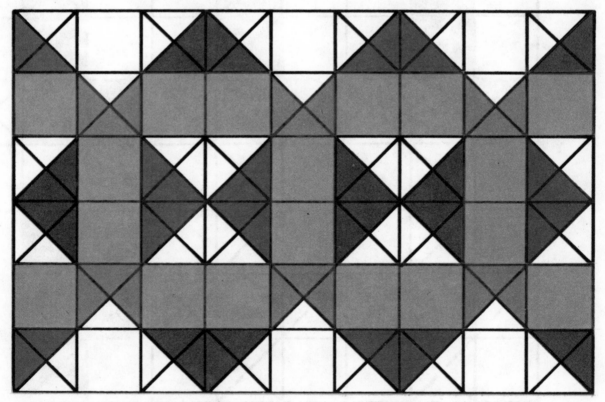

Illustration 31 **Texas Star**

Illustration 32 **Dutchman's Puzzle**

23

The four blocks in the upper left corner have been colored in a variation which requires four blocks. While each block appears to have its own central "whirly-gig"—highlighted by the contrast of the dark green against the white—attention has been focused on the reddish brown star in the center of the four blocks, a relatively large area of solid, dark color.

The motif shown at the bottom of the grid also extends beyond one block, but its combined size is smaller than that of the design in the upper left corner. Notice how the dark blue heightens the yellow star and its white center to a greater degree than does the light blue.

For our last example, we will use the **Combination Star** (*Illustration 33*). Used by itself, this is far from our favorite design. But some of the patterns which become possible when several blocks are combined are very beautiful. We have illustrated one of our favorites. Notice again that once you have decided upon your design and colored in the grid, you can determine the construction of the quilt by following the basic outline of the original block. This is possible whenever the design is based on the repetition of one block.

Illustration 33
Combination Star

Patterned fabric

The design of a patterned fabric, as well as its color, will be important to the overall effect of your patchwork quilt. Learning how to work with patterned material requires the same care and experience as does learning to work with colors.

One way to learn how to mix several patterns in one design is to study old patchwork quilts and try to understand why the maker chose the patterned fabrics used and how she determined their placement. Evaluate how well they work in the completed design.

Here are a few hints to keep in mind when using patterned fabrics:

■ *When choosing a print, consider the size of the patches into which it will be cut.* A large design may not be so pleasing if it is cut into patches so small that the design is no longer apparent.

■ *If the fabric has a bold feature, consider how to make the best use of it.* Don't destroy your patchwork design by failing to plan carefully before you cut the fabric and piece it. Stripes are an excellent example of a design element which, if used carefully, can give an exciting sense of movement, but which, if placed haphazardly, can confuse or dull the design. In **Clay's Choice** (*Illustration 34*) the central motif has been carefully planned and the stripes add to the sense of motion flowing from the center of the block. In **Clay's Choice** (*Illustration 35*) the placement of the stripes was less carefully thought out. The stripes in the corner squares do not flow from the stripes in the parallelograms, thus the sense of motion is blunted.

■ *Remember to stand back occasionally to view the sample blocks from a distance just as you will view the finished quilt top.* When deciding on colors and patterned fabrics to use in your patchwork design, you will undoubtedly work very close to the materials. However, since your finished quilt top will be viewed from a distance, it is important that you step back and look at how the fabrics interact.

■ *If you are using two fabrics which have very similar patterns, be sure that the colors are sufficiently different so that the quilt block pattern itself remains distinct.*

Illustration 34
Clay's Choice

Illustration 35
Clay's Choice

Making a grid of your finished quilt top

The grids provided for your experimentation with color and design are not large enough to represent an entire quilt top. Therefore, once you have decided which design you want to use, you should make a grid representing the quilt you intend to make. Directions for making a grid are given on page 30.

The grid will allow you to see how many times the patterns in your quilt will repeat and the relative overall scale of the design which will result. Also, as explained in the *Yardage* chapter, this grid will be very useful in determining whether to use a border on your quilt, and if so, what width to make it.

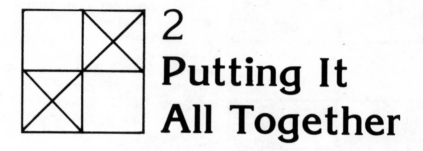

2 Putting It All Together

Planning your quilt

STANDARD QUILT SIZES

The first step in planning your quilt is deciding how large you want the finished quilt to be. To do this you must know the length and width of your mattress. You may have noticed that antique quilts are not uniform in size and are smaller than those being made today. The lack of uniformity is due to the fact that in pioneer days most beds were handmade. Also, the antique quilts are smaller because they were not intended to cover the pillows. To determine the actual length and width of your mattress, you can measure it or you can use the chart on page 27 since today mattresses are manufactured in standard sizes.

After you have determined the length and width of your mattress, it is necessary to measure the additional inches you will need to provide for the overhang (the material which extends from the top edge of the mattress to the floor). Your personal taste and the particular bedframe that supports your mattress will affect the amount of overhang you will want on your finished quilt. While most frames hold the mattress 22″ off the floor, some frames—particularly older wooden ones—are higher, and some modern platform beds rest right on the floor.

The traditional patchwork charts beginning on page 46 are calculated to produce a quilt which can serve as a full bedspread. Each quilt will cover the standard-size mattress and hang to the floor.

To develop the standard quilt sizes charted in this book, we took the standard mattress size and added 22″ to each side and to the bottom to allow for the overhang and 15″ to the top to allow for a normal-size pillow and tuck (*Illustration 36*).

Illustration 36

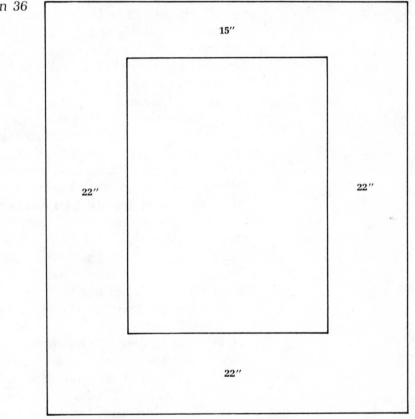

The standard sizes which result from this formula are as follows:

Standard bed and bedspread sizes

	Twin	Full	Queen	King
Mattress measurement (W/L)	39″ x 75″	54″ x 75″	60″ x 80″	72″ x 84″
Standard bedspread size (W/L)	83″ x 112″	98″ x 112″	104″ x 117″	116″ x 121″

To determine the size of your quilt, fill in the following formula:

Mattress length _____ + *Overhang* _____ + *Pillow & tuck allowance** _____ = *Quilt length* _____
Mattress width _____ + *Overhang on both sides* _____ = *Quilt width* _____

Compare the figures you have arrived at with the standard sizes and decide whether a standard size will work well for you.

If you decide on a standard size, the chart will tell you the total number of blocks needed and how many blocks long and wide the quilt top will be. The chart is arranged by standard designations (twin, full, queen, and king) and by the block sizes used in this book (12″, 15″, 16″, 18″, 20″). *Total Size* in the chart headings indicates the dimensions of the quilt top using the number of blocks of that size and in that arrangement. In developing this chart, we determined the number of whole blocks which would fit within the standard dimensions set forth above. However, not all block sizes fit neatly into the standard sizes. The easiest way to adjust the quilt top to a standard size is to add a border. The heading *Border* indicates the size border needed to make the quilt top a standard size. For example, using the 12″ block for a queen-size bed means you need 72 blocks; the quilt top will be 8 blocks wide and 9 blocks long. The total size will be 96″ by 108″. Since that is not the standard size bedspread for a queen-size bed, you may decide to add a border. To bring the quilt top up to standard size, add a border of 4″ on one side, 4″ on the other side, and 9″ at the bottom.

You may decide that the quilt size as charted will serve your needs. In some cases, a difference of a few inches in the overall width or length of the quilt may not be noticeable. A difference in length can easily be compensated for by adjusting the amount used to cover the pillows or to make the tuck. Or you may prefer to have a dust ruffle show beneath the sides and the bottom of the quilt. See directions for borders, pages 30 and 38.

MAJOR ADJUSTMENTS IN THE QUILT SIZE

To make major adjustments in the quilt size—for example, to make a crib quilt for which a standard size is not provided— use the formula which follows to determine the total number

---

* Note: If you use several pillows or pillows which are unusually large, you may want to use more than the standard 15″ for pillow and tuck allowance.

Block and border chart based on standard sizes

Twin

Block size	Total blocks (Blocks wide x Blocks long)	Total size (W/L)	Border
12″	54(6 x 9)	72″ x 108″	5½″, 5½″, 4″
15″	35(5 x 7)	75″ x 105″	4″, 4″, 7″
16″	35(5 x 7)	80″ x 112″	1½″, 1½″, 0″
18″	24(4 x 6)	72″ x 108″	5½″, 5½″, 4″
20″	20(4 x 5)	80″ x 100″	1½″, 1½″, 12″

Full

Block size	Total blocks (Blocks wide x Blocks long)	Total size (W/L)	Border
12″	72(8 x 9)	96″ x 108″	1″, 1″, 4″
15″	42(6 x 7)	90″ x 105″	4″, 4″, 7″
16″	42(6 x 7)	96″ x 112″	2″, 2″, 0″
18″	30(5 x 6)	90″ x 108″	4″, 4″, 4″
20″	20(4 x 5)	80″ x 100″	9″, 9″, 12″

Queen

Block size	Total blocks (Blocks wide x Blocks long)	Total size (W/L)	Border
12″	72(8 x 9)	96″ x 108″	4″, 4″, 9″
15″	42(6 x 7)	90″ x 105″	7″, 7″, 12″
16″	42(6 x 7)	96″ x 112″	4″, 4″, 5″
18″	30(5 x 6)	90″ x 108″	7″, 7″, 9″
20″	25(5 x 5)	100″ x 100″	2″, 2″, 17″

King

Block size	Total blocks (Blocks wide x Blocks long)	Total size (W/L)	Border
12″	90(9 x 10)	108″ x 120″	4″, 4″, 1″
15″	56(7 x 8)	105″ x 120″	5½″, 5½″, 1″
16″	49(7 x 7)	112″ x 112″	2″, 2″, 9″
18″	36(6 x 6)	108″ x 108″	4″, 4″, 13″
20″	30(5 x 6)	100″ x 120″	8″, 8″, 1″

of blocks needed and the width of the border, if any, to be used. Be sure to make a grid of your final quilt measurements, as in Illustration 37. The grid will serve as your blueprint while you are constructing your quilt.

Once you have determined the size of your finished quilt, you can figure out how many blocks of your chosen design will fit by simply dividing the width of the quilt (in inches) by the width of the block. Do the same for the length. This will give you the number of blocks needed for the width and length of the quilt. Any remainder will indicate the amount of border needed to bring the quilt top up to the size you want.

Let's take an example, using a 12″ block to make a twin-size quilt. Divide the quilt width (83″) by the block width (12″). You find that 6.9 blocks will fit in 83″. Since you will want to use only whole blocks, not partial blocks, you must determine how much of the finished width will be covered by the 6 whole blocks. Multiply 6 blocks by the size of the block (12″) and you learn that the width of 6 blocks is 72″. By subtracting 72″ from the finished width of 83″, you find that 11″ remains to be covered by the border.

Now, do the same calculation for the length. 112″ divided by 12″ equals 9.3. 9 times 12″ = 108″. Therefore, 4″ of the full length of 112″ will need to be covered by the border.

By multiplying the number of blocks needed for the width by the number of blocks needed for the length, you can determine that 54 blocks will be needed for the quilt top (6 × 9 = 54).

In adding a border to bring the quilt top up to finished standard size, you don't want all of the border to be on one side of the bed. Thus, you divide the width of the border required by 2 so that half will be on each side of the bed (11″ divided by 2 = 5½″). Because the top of the quilt will be used to cover the pillow, a border used to compensate for length is normally added only at the bottom of the quilt.

Let's make a grid of the sample quilt to show the blocks and borders. According to the figures above, we will need 54 blocks (6 across and 9 down) and a border of 5½″ on each side of the quilt and 4″ on the bottom (*Illustration 37*).

In this example the difference between the width of the side and bottom borders is so slight that you could increase the bottom border to 5½″ to make the border even around the three sides. The additional inches could be taken up by making the pillow tuck deeper. However, if the difference in border width is too great and this simple adjustment is not possible, work with the grid on other alternatives. Try changing the size of your block, the size of your quilt, or use partial or half blocks to complete the quilt or decrease border width.

Illustration 37

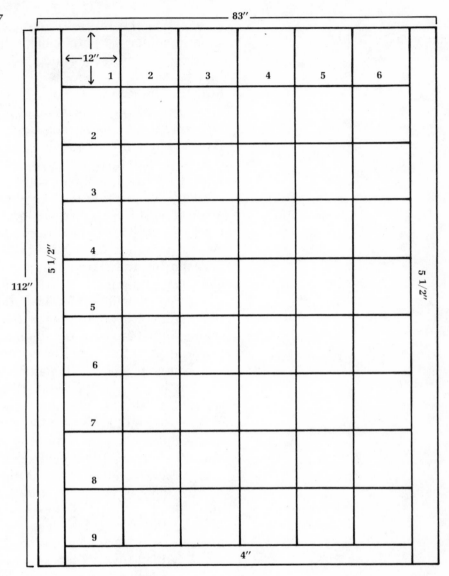

Construction techniques   MATERIALS NEEDED

For the completion of the quilt you have planned, you will need:

- fabric for the quilt top
- marking pen with indelible ink, sharpened pencil, or tailor's chalk
- fabric for the quilt lining (the underside of the quilt)
- the filling or bat
- thread and needles
- a pair of sharp dressmaker's scissors with at least 4″ blades
- a quilting hoop or frame (optional)

Selecting the fabric. A cotton or cotton blend is the best general choice for patchwork fabric. If you are not sure of the fiber content or have found a non-cotton fabric that you would love to use, think about working with the fabric and visualize how that fabric will handle. For example, you will be marking and cutting it into fairly small pieces so you will want a firm weave that will not stretch or pull easily. You will also want a fabric that will not ravel easily. Otherwise, the seams may come apart with wear. If you plan to quilt the entire surface after it is pieced, you will want a fabric that is supple and will quilt easily. Shirt or dress weight fabrics work well. Finally, try to choose fabrics that are opaque so that seam allowances and markings will not show through when the patchwork top is put against its white filling.

Preparing the fabric. Patchwork began as a way to make good use of scraps of fabric and the still-useable portions of discarded garments. Should you wish to recycle clothing into patchwork, first cut the garment apart at the seams. Discard the seams, other areas of detailed sewing, and worn spots. Then procede as outlined below for new fabric.

Fabric is prepared for patchwork just as it is for any other type of home sewing. First, it is pre-washed, to avoid later shrinkage, and tested for colorfastness. Don't let your enthusiasm tempt you to forego either step since they are both particularly important when quilting. If any material shrinks after the quilt is made, it will distort the overall design and may even break some of the quilting stitches. Obvious problems result when one color fabric of the several used in a patchwork quilt bleeds.

Once the fabric has been washed, it must be carefully pressed. Any wrinkles which flatten out after you cut the pieces will throw off the symmetry of the design.

It is important that the grain of the fabric be straight, that the vertical and horizontal threads (the warp and weft) intersect at right angles (*Illustration 38*).

Illustration 38

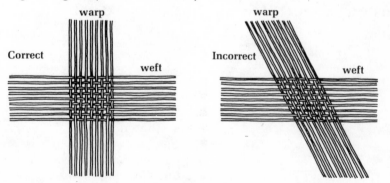

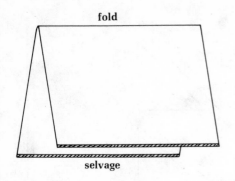

fold

selvage

Fabric off grain, edges uneven.

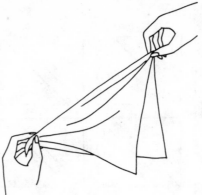

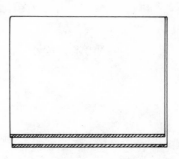

Fabric on grain, edges even.

Illustration 39

To check the grain, fold the material in half with the selvage edges together and pick it up at the fold. If the grain is straight, the raw edges will hang evenly together. If they do not, gently stretch the material from corner to corner, checking after each tug so that you don't overdo it. When the ends hang evenly, the grain is straight and you are ready to begin marking and cutting (*Illustration 39*).

Some permanent press fabrics can not be easily straightened. Be sure to check the label when you buy the fabric to learn whether it is permanent press. If it is, straighten it as much as possible and then proceed.

Cutting the fabric. The pieces for your quilt must be cut carefully, one at a time, using templates made according to the instructions in the *Template* chapter. Cutting out individual patches is not the most exciting step in the making of your quilt, but it is one of the most important. It is crucial that the cutting be done with precision. Any errors made here will result in problems later as you try to make the pieces fit together and lie flat.

Every piece should be cut with at least one side running along the "straight" of the fabric, either the warp or weft as shown in Illustration 38. Squares and triangles should be cut with two sides running along these horizontal and vertical threads whenever possible. This helps prevent the fabric from raveling and makes the piece stronger. Careful placement of the templates on the fabric also avoids waste.

The tracing may be done with tailor's chalk, light pencil, or indelible felt-tip pen. On dark fabrics, chalk generally works best. Whatever marking instrument you choose, keep it very sharp to insure accuracy.

Mark the fabric for cutting by placing the template on the wrong side of the fabric and tracing around it, with the tip of

Illustration 40

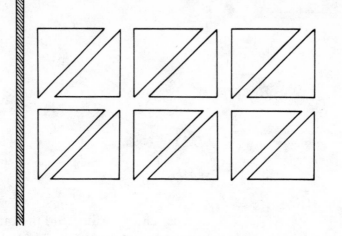

the marking instrument slanted toward rather than away from the template. This procedure is repeated until the number of pieces needed from that material for that template has been traced in even rows. Note that when tracing triangles every other template should be inverted so that the row is solid (*Illustration 40*). Be sure to allow ¼″ on each side between templates. This insures that any inaccuracy in cutting the side of one template is not transferred to the next template.

The need for accuracy also dictates that patches be cut from a single layer of fabric rather than from several layers at a time.

It is important to note that you may trace the templates for squares, triangles, and rectangles right side up or upside down. However, if you turn the template for a parallelogram upside down during your tracing, that piece will not match the ones traced when the template is right side up. Sometimes designs using parallelograms *require* that half of the total number of templates be traced one way and half the other way. Of the designs in this book, only **Ribbons** and **Columns** need both types of parallelograms. The other designs using parallelograms should all be traced with the template one way.

TIPS FOR MACHINE PIECING

Piecing the patches together to form blocks, strips, or an overall design can be easily and quickly done by machine. The only limitation machine sewing has over hand-stitching is that it is difficult to sew an L-shaped piece with an interior right angle. None of the designs in this book have interior right angles. Each may be sewn by machine using straight seams only.

We have included a seam allowance of ⅜″ in all of the

templates outlined in the *Template* chapter. Usually the seam allowances on patchwork tops are smaller than this, about $\frac{1}{4}''$. However, on most sewing machine throat plates, the smallest seam allowance marking is for $\frac{3}{8}''$. With a seam allowance of this size, you can guide your fabric along the line on the throat plate and make perfect seams.

Using the sewing machine will enable you to piece your quilt much faster than you could by hand. While this mechanization is a great time saver, it also lends itself to error. Be careful to make your seam allowances exactly $\frac{3}{8}''$ or you will have great difficulty in setting your finished blocks together.

When you are piecing shapes with diagonal edges, such as triangles and parallelograms, positioning them for sewing requires a little experimentation. If you match the cut edges, then stitch and press, the ends of the seam won't match. Match the *seam line,* not the cut edge. Once you have done one of these correctly, use it as a model for all other similar pieces in the quilt top (*Illustration 41*).

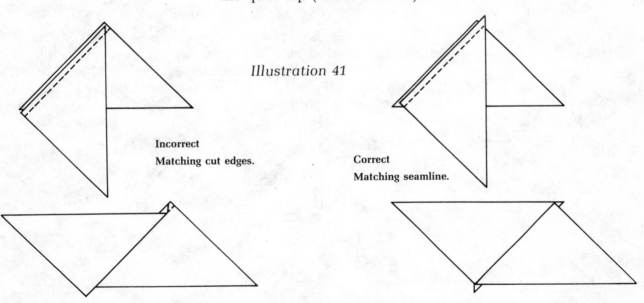

Illustration 41

Incorrect

Matching cut edges.

Correct

Matching seamline.

CONSTRUCTING THE BLOCKS

Since the thread used to construct the blocks will not be visible, you need not change the color of the thread to correspond to the material you are working with. Choose one color that will blend with the entire design.

Size 50 cotton thread may be used, but cotton-wrapped polyester is preferable for its greater strength. The length of the stitch is determined by balancing the need for strength against

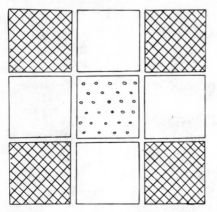

Step 1

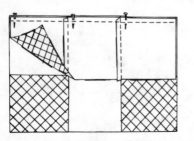

Step 2

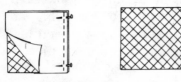

Step 3

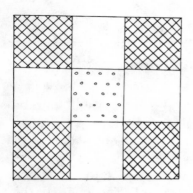

Illustration 42

the possibility that you may make some mistakes that you will want to remove. Ten to twelve stitches to the inch usually work well.

Assembling blocks containing only one size and shape template. A **Nine-Patch** (page 52) is the simplest block of all to sew together. Simply join each horizontal row of three squares to form a strip. Then join the three strips to form the finished block (*Illustration 42*).

The next simplest block is that composed of eight right triangles. (See **Sugar Bowl,** page 46.) Begin by joining each set of corner triangles to form a square. Then sew the seams between the two squares to form a row. Finally, join the two rows to complete the block (*Illustration 43*).

Assembling blocks containing more than one shape and size template. The technique for joining any multiple-template block is the same and can be summarized in two basic rules:

1 Join the smallest pieces first.

2 Plan the construction so that only straight seams are necessary.

The process is basically the same as that used in constructing the block using right triangles. Always begin by combining smaller pieces to form squares and joining the squares to form strips. Then join the strips to complete the block. We have illustrated this process using the **Prairie Queen** block design (*Illustration 44*).

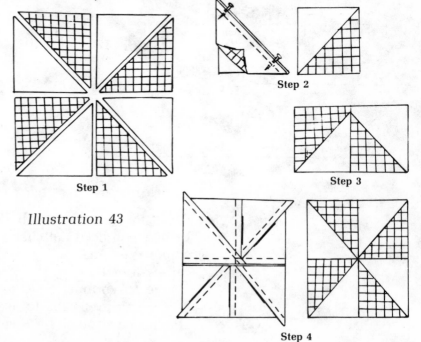

Step 1

Step 2

Step 3

Step 4

Illustration 43

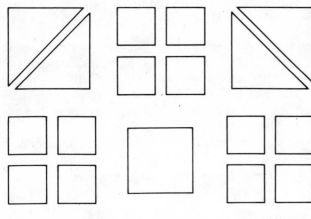

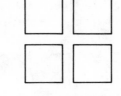

Step 1

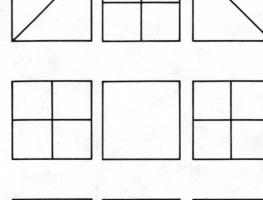
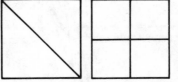

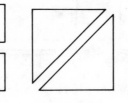

Step 2

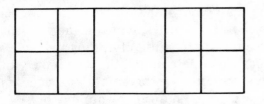
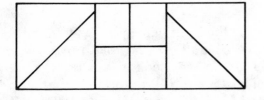
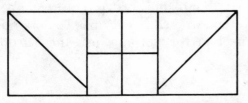

Step 3

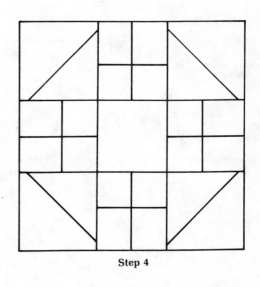

Step 4

Illustration 44

37

General pointers. The following general pointers apply, regardless of the type of block you are constructing:

■ Accuracy in sewing is the necessary counterpart to precision in cutting. Piecing is not difficult, but don't be lulled into carelessness.
■ Since each seam will be crossed by another line of stitching as the blocks are joined, it is not necessary to lock the thread by back-stitching at the start and end of each seam. To speed up the process even more, sew pieces together with one continuous thread, allowing enough space between each pair for the thread to be cut (*Illustration 45*).

Illustration 45

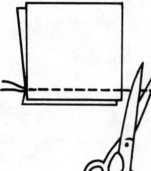

■ Always press a seam before sewing across it. Press seams to one side, rather than open. Plan your pressing so that the allowances of seams which intersect are pressed in opposite directions.

SETTING THE QUILT

In quilting jargon, "setting the quilt" means sewing the blocks together to form the overall pattern (the "set") of the quilt.

In a procedure similar to the one used for construction of the individual block, the blocks are joined to form strips, then the strips joined together to form the completed top. Since it is important to the design that the seams joining the blocks intersect precisely, you may want to hand-baste the intersections and ease the fabric to fit before sewing on the machine.

Borders. Borders are added to the quilt after the top is set. As noted previously, the easiest way to adjust the length or width of your quilt is to use a border. Use the charts on page 29 to determine the standard size for your quilt, the number of blocks and their arrangement for the block size you have chosen, the total size of your quilt top, and the border requirements to bring the quilt top up to standard bedspread size. To determine the amount of fabric needed for borders, use the *Yardage Charts*.

ASSEMBLING THE QUILT

The three pieces which you will be working with once you have set the quilt and added the border, if any, are the com-

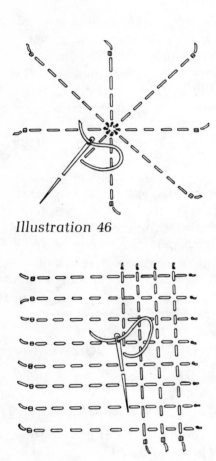

Illustration 46

Illustration 47

pleted quilt top, the filling, and the lining. The lining, or underside of the quilt, may be made from any complimentary fabric of your choice. You may wish to use a sheet and avoid having any seams.

The filling most commonly used today is polyester batting, which is available in sheets designed for standard-size bedspreads. Polyester bat has the tremendous advantage of holding its shape during use and cleaning so that it does not have to be quilted so finely as the traditional cotton bat. Cotton batting becomes lumpy with use, so that quilting must be close together to hold the cotton in place. When cotton batting is used for the filling, the lines of stitching should be no more than 2″ apart. On old quilts, they are often an inch or less apart. There can be a great deal more space between the lines of stitching when a polyester bat is used. Three inches is a fairly standard width. Thus the polyester bat allows greater freedom of design and requires less time for the quilting stage. A wool bat may be used when greater warmth is desired, but the wool bat is generally too thick for quilting and is tied instead. See page 41. You may also wish to consider using an old blanket for the filling.

To assemble the quilt, place the lining on a clean surface, right side down, then cover it with the bat, and smooth it. Finally, cover the bat with the quilt top, right side up. Smooth all of the layers and fasten them together with several large safety pins to keep the materials from shifting. Hand-baste the layers together, beginning at the center and working out to the sides, then from the center to the corners, and finally around the edges of the quilt. Or you may want to start the basting in the center and work two lines from side to side and then two lines from top to bottom, completing the grid in the same pattern (*Illustrations 46 and 47*).

QUILTING

Depending on your resources of both time and space, you have several choices of how to quilt your patchwork:

Quilting on a frame. Traditionally, quilting was done on a frame as wide as the quilt. The lining was sewn to the bars of the frame and clamps were used to hold the work in place. Today frames may be full quilt size or may require rolling the ends of the quilt around bars, out of the way, leaving exposed only that part of the quilt which is being worked on.

Quilting with a hoop. Quilting hoops are also available. Much larger than embroidery hoops, they allow you to work

Illustration 48

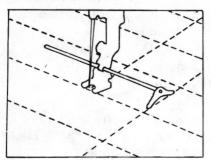

Illustration 49

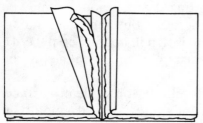

Illustration 50

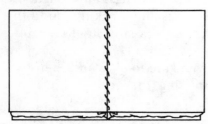

on one section at a time, although the entire quilt will be spread out around you. As in the basting step, the quilt is worked from the center out. Since the material may shift, the basting threads may have to be cut at some points as you progress.

Quilting by machine. Quilting may also be done on a machine but this is not as easy as it may sound. Remember the size of the piece you are working with, both its surface area and its bulk. If you have a quilting foot for your machine, the going may be somewhat easier (*Illustration 48*). If you quilt by machine, the initial basting that you do becomes even more important because of the increased problem you will have in keeping the layers together as you feed the material through the machine.

Quilting by the block. It is possible to quilt each block individually, thus having to work with the bulk of the entire quilt only at the final stage. To do this, take each completed block (or set of four blocks, or whatever number of blocks you find manageable) and follow the general instructions given above for assembling and quilting the quilt top. After all of the pieces are quilted (see the general directions for quilting which follow), join them by machine sewing the pieced top layer of the blocks together, then trim the filling pieces so they just touch and do not overlap (*Illustration 49*). Finally, turn under the seam allowance of the lining and whipstitch (*Illustration 50*).

QUILTING DESIGNS

You have as much range with the choice of the quilting design as with the block design itself. The most traditional and perhaps the easiest method is to outline each piece in the quilt with a row of stitching on either side of each seam, $\frac{1}{8}''$ to $\frac{1}{4}''$ away. Overall designs of squares and diamonds may also be done quite simply. Fancy quilting stencils—of feathers and flowers and scrolls, for example—are available from several sources and outlines from which you can create your own stencils can be found in many quilting books.

The quilting stitch is merely a fine running stitch done with as much precision and regularity as you can manage. Some needleworkers find that it is best done with one hand below the quilt to guide the needle. You may also find that it works better to sew toward your body rather than away from it. Do what suits you best.

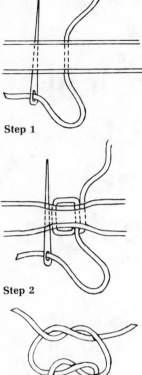

Step 1

Step 2

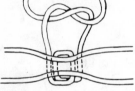

Step 3

Illustration 51

TIEING

If you are using a heavy wool bat for the filling, you may want to tie the layers of the quilt together rather than quilt them. Assemble the quilt and select evenly-spaced points on the quilt top—perhaps suggested by the design of the block. Double thread a tapestry needle with yarn and, leaving about two inches of yarn free above the fabric, make two stitches in the same spot. Tie two firm knots and trim the yarn to an even length. This will create a decorative tuft of yarn to conceal the knot (*Illustration 51*).

FINISHING

After the blocks are set together, the edges are finished (just like a regular quilt) in one of the following ways:

Fold a narrow edge of the backing over the front; turn under, and hem by hand (*Illustration 52*).

Fold a narrow edge of the top over the backing in the opposite direction; turn under, and hem by hand (*Illustration 53*).

Fold the edge of both the top and the backing into the center and stitch together with two rows of small even stitches: one row just below the fold, and the second about $\frac{1}{4}''$ away. (*Illustration 54*).

Bind the edges with double-fold bias tape either purchased or made of one of the patchwork fabrics. This is the easiest to replace when the edges get worn (*Illustration 55*).

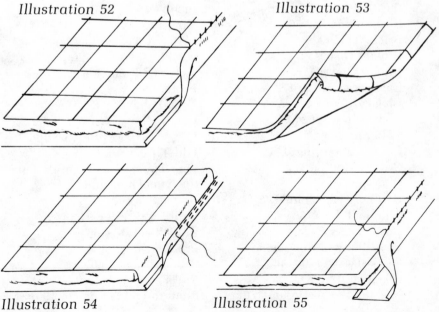

Illustration 52

Illustration 53

Illustration 54

Illustration 55

Alphabetical Listing of Traditional Quilt Designs in Book

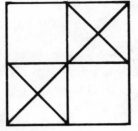

3
50 Traditional Patchwork Designs with 100 Color and Design Variations

The basic unit of each patchwork pattern is the block—the design element which is repeated throughout the quilt top. Each block is made up of individual pieces of cloth called patches. The basic format of the design is determined by the number of patches running along each side of the block. For example, a three-patch design has three patches across each side. (Often, the total number of patches is used for the name instead—a three-patch then becomes a nine-patch since there are nine patches in the entire block.) In this book, we have chosen to use only three- and four-patch blocks that can be sewn by machine as well as by hand.

Beginning with **Sugar Bowl,** which contains only eight patches in each block, and ending with **Combination Star,** which has 41 patches, the designs presented in this chapter progress from easy, fast projects to more challenging, time-consuming projects.

It is interesting to see the design tradition of the patchwork quilt in its historical context. Patchwork is a uniquely American art form, which developed in the early days of the nation when cloth was imported and was therefore very expensive and difficult to obtain. Women used their carefully saved scraps to mend their bedding. Eventually they began to use the scraps to create patterned quilt tops, many of them based on the use of repeated blocks, each block composed of several individual pieces of fabric. At first, each block design was unique to the person making the quilt. To distinguish her design from everyone else's, she gave it a name. The block designs were exchanged among friends and then carried to new geographic areas as people moved westward. During this process, the block designs were often altered slightly and named anew. And as time passed and people's lives changed, the block designs came to represent new facets of their lives and the old blocks were renamed. This explains why so many patchwork designs are known by several different names and why so many designs are reminiscent of others.

The fifty patchwork block designs introduced in this chapter are all old-time patchwork favorites. Each design is illustrated on a two-page spread containing the following:

■ the traditional name of the block
■ a short historical note
■ the block in its traditional configuration, with the usual number of colors and placement of light and dark colors (The traditional configuration is the *top* block of the three shown.)
■ two illustrations of the block with non-traditional placement of light and dark colors, suggesting the large number of variations possible
■ three template charts—for 12″, 16″ and 20″ blocks in four-patch designs, and for 12″, 15″ and 18″ blocks in three-patch designs—keyed to any one of the four standard bedspread sizes and indicating the total number of pieces needed to make the quilt top
■ a large grid containing twelve blocks placed side by side for your use in experimenting with your own color choices and color placement.

To try out your colors on the large grid, you can either color directly on the page using colored pencils or on tracing paper placed over the grid. Tracing paper allows you to try several possibilities on the same grid. Remember that while the grid contains enough blocks to give you an idea of what the overall quilt top design will look like, it is not an exact representation of the whole quilt top. The actual number of blocks used for your quilt will be determined by the size block you choose to use and the size bedspread you choose to make.

The following is an explanation of how you can use the template chart to make your quilt in one of the traditional patterns:

ⓐ 12″ block

ⓑ Templates	ⓒ Color	ⓓ Code	ⓔ Number of pieces needed for quilt			
			Twin	Full	Queen	King
△	*white*	T10	216	288	288	360
△	*blue*	T10	216	288	288	360
		Totals	432	576	576	720

ⓕ (totals row bracket)

a The possible block sizes are determined by the block design: three-patch designs may be done in 12″, 15″, and 18″ blocks; four-patch designs may be done in 12″, 16″, and 20″ blocks. The larger the block, the less work you will have to do to make your quilt.

b This column shows the shape of the templates used.

c This column states the color of the piece used in the traditional block design.

d The template code indicates exactly which of the templates outlined in the *Template* chapter will be needed. An explanation of the code is found on page 200.

e These columns show the number of pieces for each template in each color needed to make a quilt in the four standard sizes.

f The totals for each column enable you to judge how time-consuming making a quilt in this block size will be. The more templates, the more pieces to cut, the more seams to sew, and the more time-consuming the project will be. Depending upon your patience, here are some guidelines: 250–500 templates is a good beginner's project, 500–750 is intermediate, anything over that will take a good deal of time but, if done well, will be a masterpiece!

If you use one of the illustrated variations or an original design, the information provided for the traditional design in the Template Chart can be developed by using the *Designer's Worksheet,* page 193.

The variations we illustrate only begin to suggest the possible variations for each block—so don't choose your favorite until you have tried several!

Sugar Bowl

The first of a number of designs illustrated in this book which were named after common household items, this design represents a prized possession which was carefully brought westward by the pioneers. Templates which are easy to cut and simple to piece make this design perfect for a beginner's project.

12″ block

Templates	Color	Code	Number of pieces needed for quilt			
			Twin	Full	Queen	King
△	white	T10	216	288	288	360
△	blue	T10	216	288	288	360
		Totals	432	576	576	720

16″ block

Templates	Color	Code	Number of pieces needed for quilt			
			Twin	Full	Queen	King
△	white	T12*	140	168	168	196
△	blue	T12*	140	168	168	196
		Totals	280	336	336	392

20″ block

Templates	Color	Code	Number of pieces needed for quilt			
			Twin	Full	Queen	King
△	white	T13*	80	80	100	120
△	blue	T13*	80	80	100	120
		Totals	160	160	200	240

*Template outline not provided.

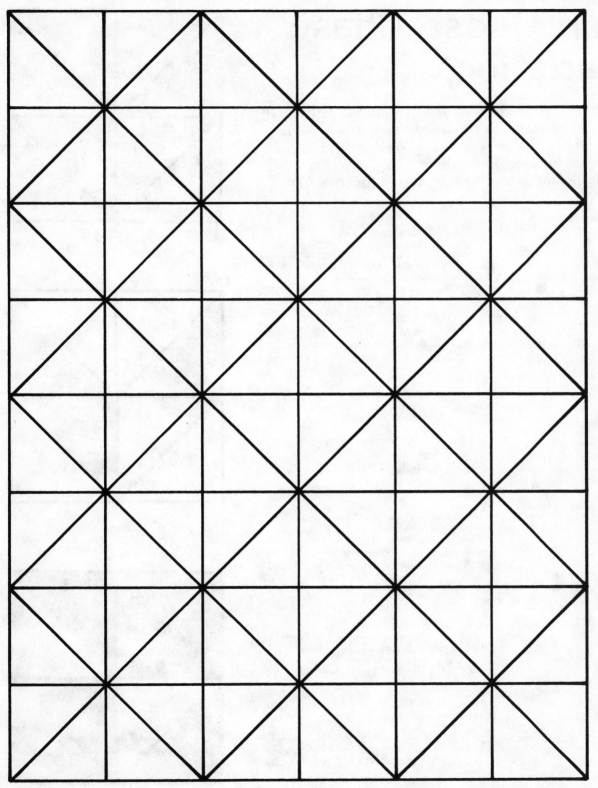

4-patch

Total pieces in block: 8

Wild Goose Chase (Variation)

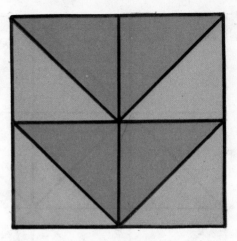

This block is a variation of **Wild Goose Chase (Overall Designs,** page 181). The traditional design is comprised of triangles of two sizes and is worked in bold, contrasting colors. Many new and exciting effects can be achieved with this variation of an old favorite.

12″ block

Templates	Color	Code	Number of pieces needed for quilt			
			Twin	Full	Queen	King
△	light orange	T10	216	288	288	360
△	dark orange	T10	216	288	288	360
		Totals	432	576	576	720

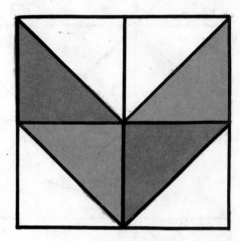

16″ block

Templates	Color	Code	Number of pieces needed for quilt			
			Twin	Full	Queen	King
△	light orange	T12*	140	168	168	196
△	dark orange	T12*	140	168	168	196
		Totals	280	336	336	392

20″ block

Templates	Color	Code	Number of pieces needed for quilt			
			Twin	Full	Queen	King
△	light orange	T13*	80	80	100	120
△	dark orange	T13*	80	80	100	120
		Totals	160	160	200	240

*Template outline not provided.

4-patch

Total pieces in block: 8

Broken Dishes

When the pioneer women travelled to the West in their covered wagons, they usually carried along a set of dishes to remind them of home. When these dishes broke they could not easily be replaced—hence, the name of this design commemorates one of life's small catastrophes.

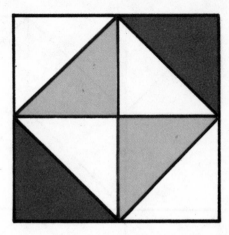

12" block

Templates	Color	Code	Number of pieces needed for quilt			
			Twin	Full	Queen	King
△	pink	T10	108	144	144	180
△	dark blue	T10	108	144	144	180
△	white	T10	216	288	288	360
		Totals	432	576	576	720

16" block

Templates	Color	Code	Number of pieces needed for quilt			
			Twin	Full	Queen	King
△	pink	T12*	70	84	84	98
△	dark blue	T12*	70	84	84	98
△	white	T12*	140	168	168	196
		Totals	280	336	336	392

20" block

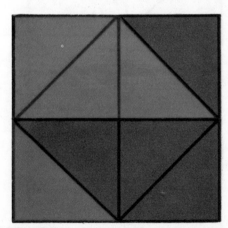

Templates	Color	Code	Number of pieces needed for quilt			
			Twin	Full	Queen	King
△	pink	T13*	40	40	50	60
△	dark blue	T13*	40	40	50	60
△	white	T13*	80	80	100	120
		Totals	160	160	200	240

*Template outline not provided.

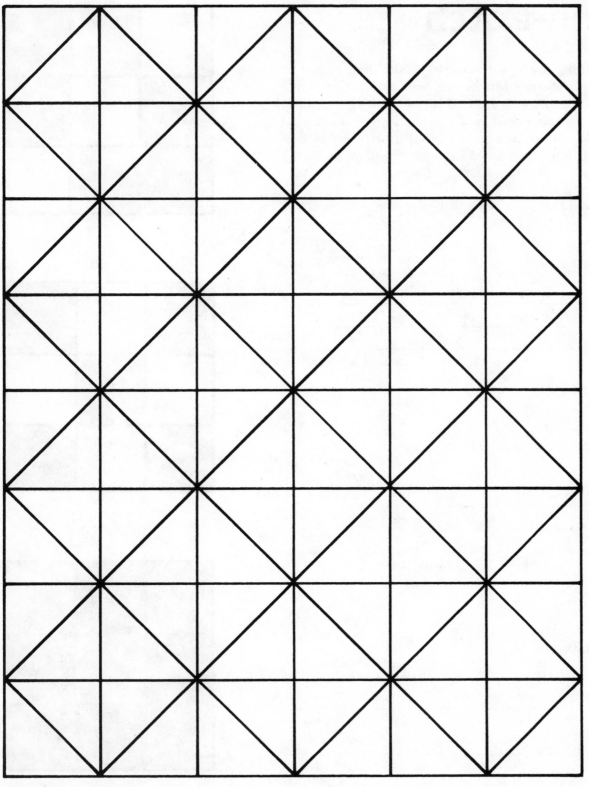

4-patch

Total pieces in block: 8

Nine-Patch

Originating in Massachussetts, **Nine-Patch** *is one of the easiest patchwork blocks and was often used when teaching young girls how to piece their first quilt. Although the block is a very simple design, if colors are carefully chosen, beautiful overall patterns can be achieved when the blocks are set together in a quilt top.*

Also illustrated in the **Overall Design** *chapter, page 185.*

12″ block

Templates	Color	Code	Number of pieces needed for quilt			
			Twin	Full	Queen	King
☐	orange	S4	324	432	432	540
☐	white	S4	162	216	216	270
		Totals	486	648	648	810

15″ block

Templates	Color	Code	Number of pieces needed for quilt			
			Twin	Full	Queen	King
☐	orange	S5	210	252	252	336
☐	white	S5	105	126	126	168
		Totals	315	378	378	504

18″ block

Templates	Color	Code	Number of pieces needed for quilt			
			Twin	Full	Queen	King
☐	orange	S6	144	180	180	216
☐	white	S6	72	90	90	108
		Totals	216	270	270	324

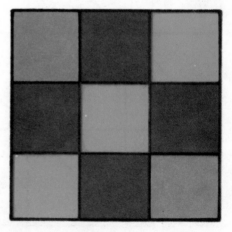

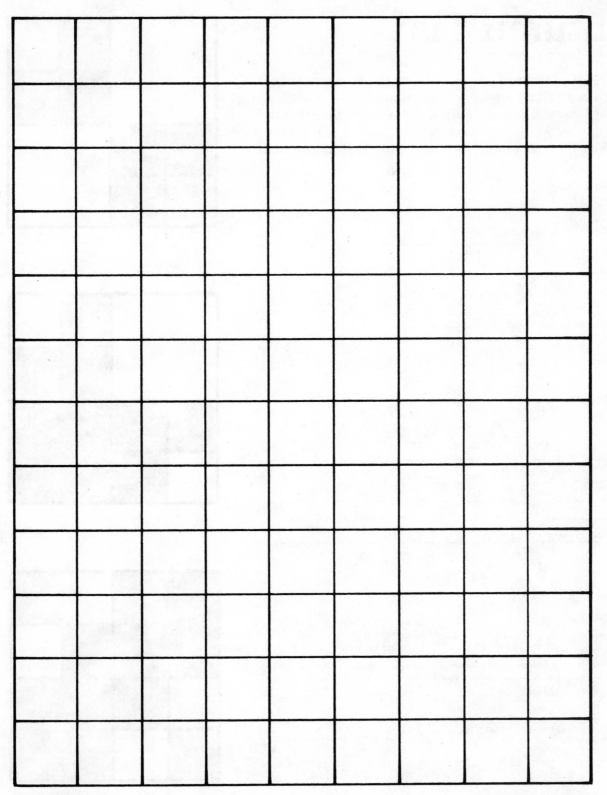

3-patch

Total pieces in block: 9

Autumn Tints

Nature played an important role in the lives of early Americans. This pattern is one example of the way Nature's beauty influenced patchwork design. But Nature has her malevolent side as well and this too was reflected in design names such as **Streak-of-Lightning**.

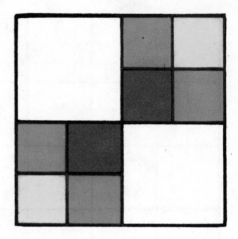

12" block

Templates	Color	Code	Number of pieces needed for quilt			
			Twin	Full	Queen	King
☐	brown	S3	108	144	144	180
☐	orange	S3	216	288	288	360
☐	yellow	S3	108	144	144	180
☐	white	S6	108	144	144	180
		Totals	540	720	720	900

16" block

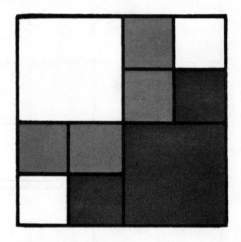

Templates	Color	Code	Number of pieces needed for quilt			
			Twin	Full	Queen	King
☐	brown	S4	70	84	84	98
☐	orange	S4	140	168	168	196
☐	yellow	S4	70	84	84	98
☐	white	S7	70	84	84	98
		Totals	350	420	420	490

20" block

Templates	Color	Code	Number of pieces needed for quilt			
			Twin	Full	Queen	King
☐	brown	S5	40	40	50	60
☐	orange	S5	80	80	100	120
☐	yellow	S5	40	40	50	60
☐	white	S8	40	40	50	60
		Totals	200	200	250	300

4-patch

Total pieces in block: 10

Birds-in-the-Air

One of the earliest colonial patchwork designs, this design was a favorite because each square may be cut from different material. In the days when fabric was imported and very precious, this design made good use of all the carefully saved fabric scraps.

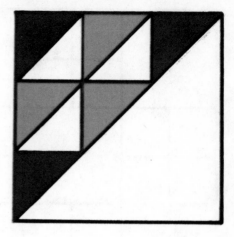

12″ block

Templates	Color	Code	Number of pieces needed for quilt			
			Twin	Full	Queen	King
△	gray	T6	162	216	216	270
△	pink	T6	162	216	216	270
△	white	T6	162	216	216	270
△	white	T14*	54	72	72	90
		Totals	540	720	720	900

15″ block

Templates	Color	Code	Number of pieces needed for quilt			
			Twin	Full	Queen	King
△	gray	T8	105	126	126	168
△	pink	T8	105	126	126	168
△	white	T8	105	126	126	168
△	white	T15*	35	42	42	56
		Totals	350	420	420	560

18″ block

Templates	Color	Code	Number of pieces needed for quilt			
			Twin	Full	Queen	King
△	gray	T10	72	90	90	108
△	pink	T10	72	90	90	108
△	white	T10	72	90	90	108
△	white	T16*	24	30	30	36
		Totals	240	300	300	360

*Template outline not provided.

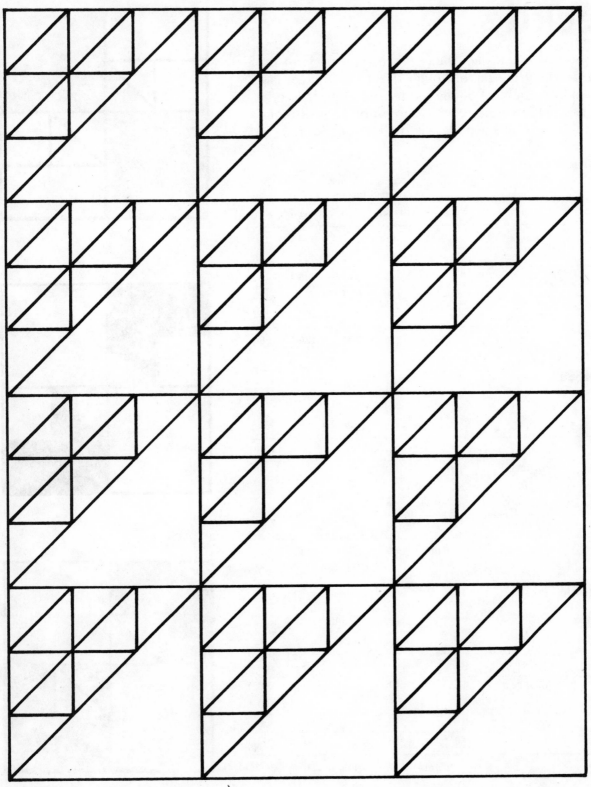

3-patch

Total pieces in block: 10

Necktie

The center of this design looks much like the knot in a western-style string tie, although the overall effect is much more suggestive of the modern bowtie. It is interesting to note that one recent innovation in quiltmaking is the use of old neckties as a source of fabric.

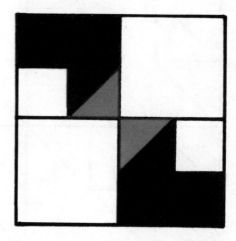

12″ block

Templates	Color	Code	Number of pieces needed for quilt			
			Twin	Full	Queen	King
□	blue	S6	108	144	144	180
△	orange	T4	108	144	144	180
□	white	S3	108	144	144	180
▭	white	R3	108	144	144	180
△	white	T4	108	144	144	180
		Totals	540	720	720	900

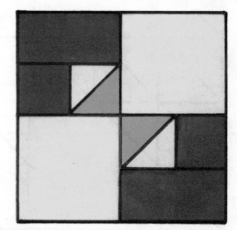

16″ block

Templates	Color	Code	Number of pieces needed for quilt			
			Twin	Full	Queen	King
□	blue	S7	70	84	84	98
△	orange	T6	70	84	84	98
□	white	S4	70	84	84	98
▭	white	R4	70	84	84	98
△	white	T6	70	84	84	98
		Totals	350	420	420	490

20″ block

Templates	Color	Code	Number of pieces needed for quilt			
			Twin	Full	Queen	King
□	blue	S8	40	40	50	60
△	orange	T8	40	40	50	60
□	white	S5	40	40	50	60
▭	white	R6	40	40	50	60
△	white	T8	40	40	50	60
		Totals	200	200	250	300

4-patch

Total pieces in block: 10

Hour Glass

The design configuration in this block clearly represents that old, familiar timer, the hour glass. Variations of this motif are seen in other patchwork patterns like **Ohio Star, Letter X, Cat and Mice,** and **Joseph's Coat.**

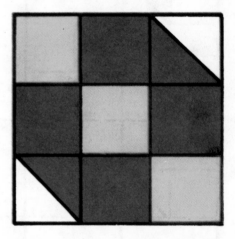

12″ block

Templates	Color	Code	Twin	Full	Queen	King
			Number of pieces needed for quilt			
□	brown	S4	216	288	288	360
□	pink	S4	108	144	144	180
△	pink	T6	108	144	144	180
□	white	S4	54	72	72	90
△	white	T6	108	144	144	180
		Totals	594	792	792	990

15″ block

Templates	Color	Code	Twin	Full	Queen	King
			Number of pieces needed for quilt			
□	brown	S5	140	168	168	224
□	pink	S5	70	84	84	112
△	pink	T8	70	84	84	112
□	white	S5	35	42	42	56
△	white	T8	70	84	84	112
		Totals	385	462	462	616

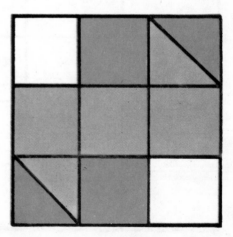

18″ block

Templates	Color	Code	Twin	Full	Queen	King
			Number of pieces needed for quilt			
□	brown	S6	96	120	120	144
□	pink	S6	48	60	60	72
△	pink	T10	48	60	60	72
□	white	S6	24	30	30	36
△	white	T10	48	60	60	72
		Totals	264	330	330	396

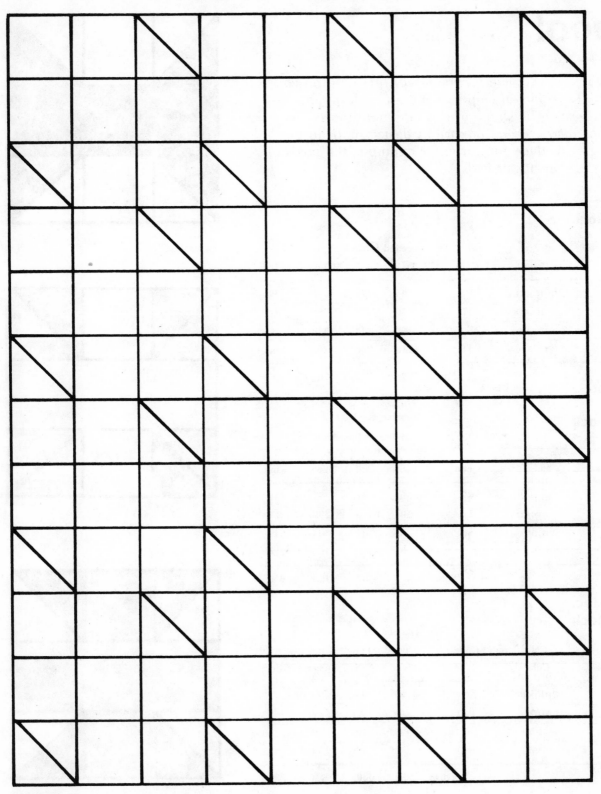

3-patch

Total pieces in block: 11

Spool

You would expect every person working with patch-work to have lots of empty spools—the shape this design suggests. The shape of this common household item has also been an important design motif in the making of wooden furniture; for example, the posts of many old four-poster beds.

12″ block

Templates	Color	Code	Number of pieces needed for quilt			
			Twin	Full	Queen	King
▭	maroon	R5	54	72	72	90
△	maroon	T6	216	288	288	360
□	white	S4	108	144	144	180
△	white	T6	216	288	288	360
		Totals	594	792	792	990

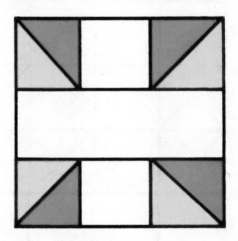

15″ block

Templates	Color	Code	Number of Pieces needed for quilt			
			Twin	Full	Queen	King
▭	maroon	R7	35	42	42	56
△	maroon	T8	140	168	168	224
□	white	S5	70	84	84	112
△	white	T8	140	168	168	224
		Totals	385	462	462	616

18″ block

Templates	Color	Code	Number of pieces needed for quilt			
			Twin	Full	Queen	King
▭	maroon	R8	24	30	30	36
△	maroon	T10	96	120	120	144
□	white	S6	48	60	60	72
△	white	T10	96	120	120	144
		Totals	264	330	330	396

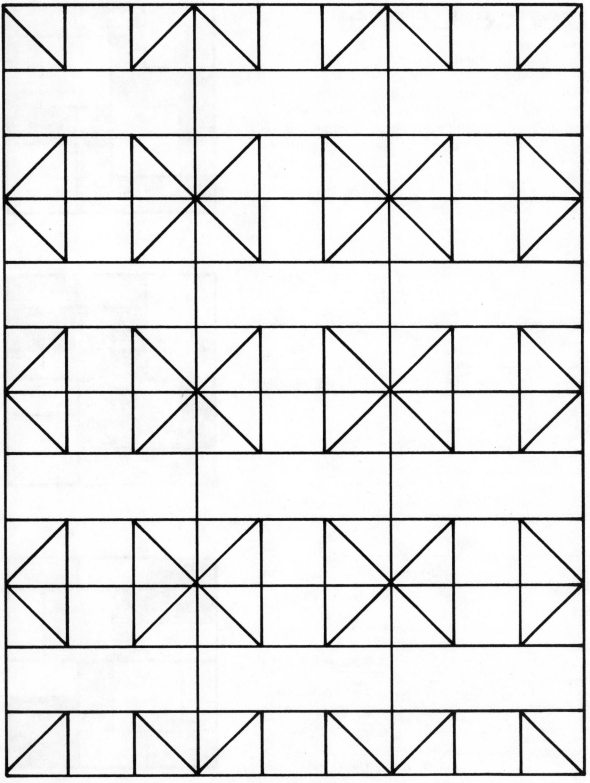

3-patch

Total pieces in block: 11

Patience Corner

This design was traditionally pieced using L-shaped templates and squares. The L-shaped templates are impossible to piece by machine and extremely difficult to piece by hand. Although piecing this design takes a great deal of time and patience (hence its name), it was popular in the last half of the eighteenth century. The block illustrated here has been adapted so that it may be easily pieced by machine.

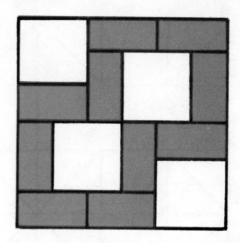

12″ block

Templates	Color	Code	Number of pieces needed for quilt			
			Twin	Full	Queen	King
▭	red	R1	540	720	720	900
▢	white	S4	216	288	288	360
		Totals	756	1,008	1,008	1,260

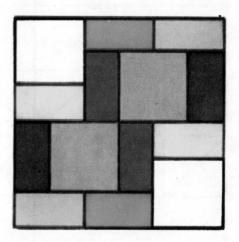

15″ block

Templates	Color	Code	Number of pieces needed for quilt			
			Twin	Full	Queen	King
▭	red	R2	350	420	420	560
▢	white	S5	140	168	168	224
		Totals	490	588	588	784

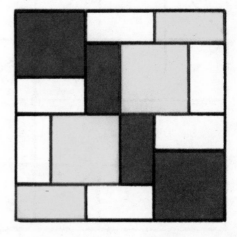

18″ block

Templates	Color	Code	Number of pieces needed for quilt			
			Twin	Full	Queen	King
▭	red	R3	240	300	300	360
▢	white	S6	96	120	120	144
		Totals	336	420	420	504

3-patch

Total pieces in block: 14

Shoo-Fly

Shoo-fly is a phrase made familiar to many of us by the old Civil War nonsense song "Shoo-fly, Don't Bother Me", or by Shoo-fly pie (an open pie with a filling of molasses and brown sugar). This design is also called **Star Spangled Banner** *when done in red, white, and blue and* **Chinese Coin** *when done in green and yellow on white.*

12″ block

Templates	Color	Code	Number of pieces needed for quilt			
			Twin	Full	Queen	King
△	green	T6	216	288	288	360
□	green	S4	54	72	72	90
△	white	T6	216	288	288	360
□	white	S4	216	288	288	360
		Totals	**702**	**936**	**936**	**1,170**

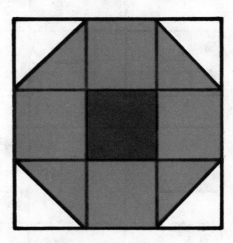

15″ block

Templates	Color	Code	Number of pieces needed for quilt			
			Twin	Full	Queen	King
△	green	T8	140	168	168	224
□	green	S5	35	42	42	56
△	white	T8	140	168	168	224
□	white	S5	140	168	168	224
		Totals	**455**	**546**	**546**	**728**

18″ block

Templates	Color	Code	Number of pieces needed for quilt			
			Twin	Full	Queen	King
△	green	T10	96	120	120	144
□	green	S6	24	30	30	36
△	white	T10	96	120	120	144
□	white	S6	96	120	120	144
		Totals	**312**	**390**	**390**	**468**

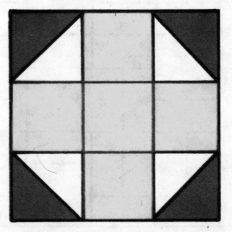

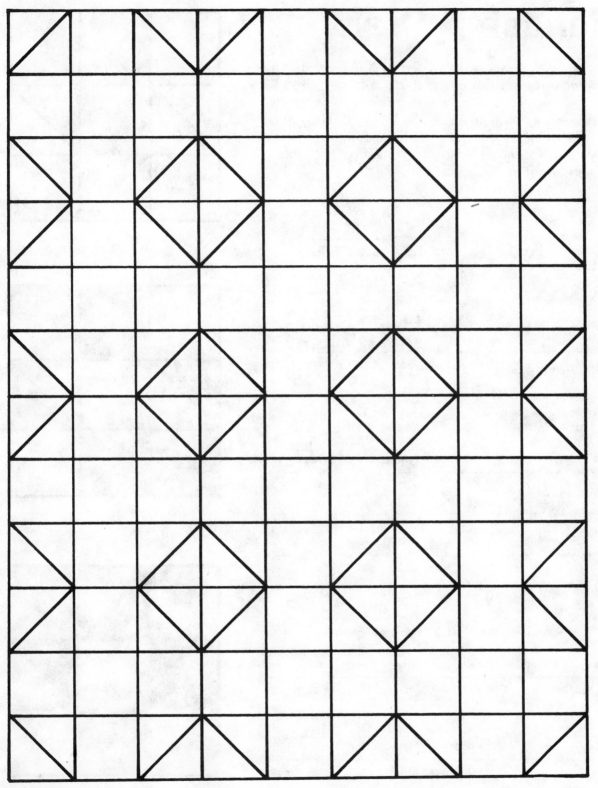

3-patch

Total pieces in block: 13

Friendship Star

In pioneer days, quilts were pieced at home during the long winter days and set and quilted with a group of friends and neighbors at a "quilting bee" in the spring. **Friendship Star** commemorates these friends who not only helped with each other's quilts, but also traded fabric scraps so that each had more colors available for her next quilt.

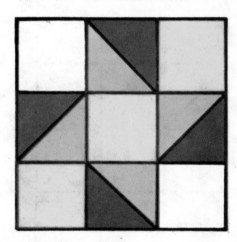

12" block

Templates	Color	Code	Twin	Full	Queen	King
			Number of pieces needed for quilt			
□	blue	S4	54	72	72	90
△	blue	T6	216	288	288	360
□	white	S4	216	288	288	360
△	white	T6	216	288	288	360
		Totals	702	936	936	1,170

15" block

Templates	Color	Code	Twin	Full	Queen	King
			Number of pieces needed for quilt			
□	blue	S5	35	42	42	56
△	blue	T8	140	168	168	224
□	white	S5	140	168	168	224
△	white	T8	140	168	168	224
		Totals	455	546	546	728

18" block

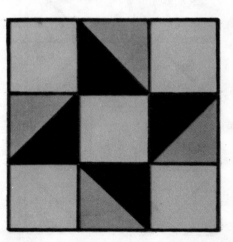

Templates	Color	Code	Twin	Full	Queen	King
			Number of pieces needed for quilt			
□	blue	S6	24	30	30	36
△	blue	T10	96	120	120	144
□	white	S6	96	120	120	144
△	white	T10	96	120	120	144
		Totals	312	390	390	468

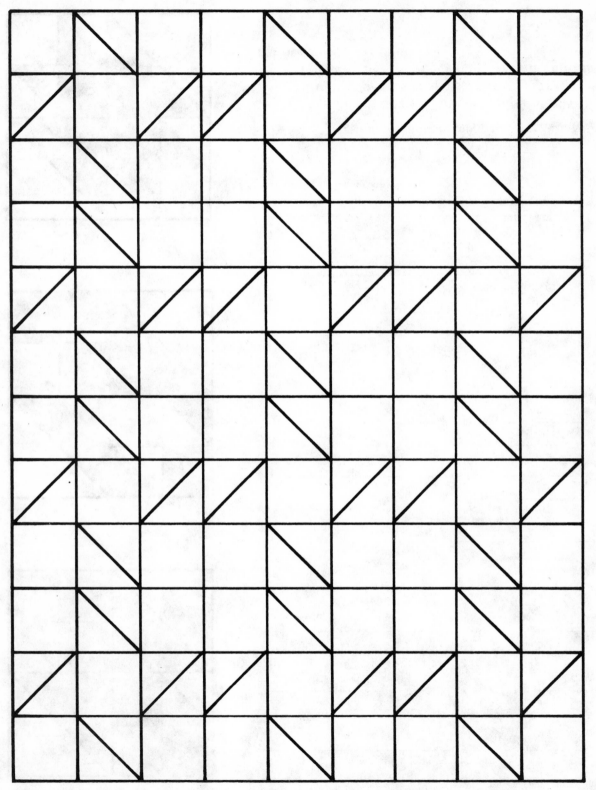

3-patch

Total pieces in block: 13

The Anvil

Women often named their designs after commonplace things. This design represents the anvil which most farmers had handy to make and repair metal tools.

Also shown in **Rotated Block** *chapter, page 171.*

12" block

Templates	Color	Code	Number of pieces needed for quilt			
			Twin	Full	Queen	King
△	blue	T10	108	144	144	180
☐	blue	S3	108	144	144	180
△	blue	T4	216	288	288	360
△	white	T10	108	144	144	180
☐	white	S3	108	144	144	180
△	white	T4	216	288	288	360
		Totals	**864**	**1,152**	**1,152**	**1,440**

16" block

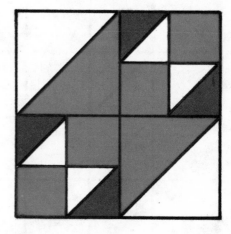

Templates	Color	Code	Number of pieces needed for quilt			
			Twin	Full	Queen	King
△	blue	T12*	70	84	84	98
☐	blue	S4	70	84	84	98
△	blue	T6	140	168	168	196
△	white	T12*	70	84	84	98
☐	white	S4	70	84	84	98
△	white	T6	140	168	168	196
		Totals	**560**	**672**	**672**	**784**

20" block

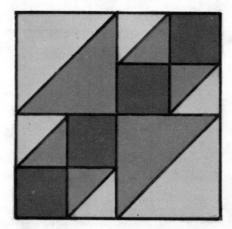

Templates	Color	Code	Number of pieces needed for quilt			
			Twin	Full	Queen	King
△	blue	T13*	40	40	50	60
☐	blue	S5	40	40	50	60
△	blue	T8	80	80	100	120
△	white	T13*	40	40	50	60
☐	white	S5	40	40	50	60
△	white	T8	80	80	100	120
		Totals	**320**	**320**	**400**	**480**

*Template outline not provided.

4-patch

Total pieces in block: 16

Yankee Puzzle

This pattern was a favorite of the Yankees in New York and the New England states. Actually, in Revolutionary times, the term "Yankees" was used to distinguish those who supported the Revolution from those who favored the Crown. Only during the Civil War did it come to denote a northerner.

12″ block

Templates	Color	Code	Number of pieces needed for quilt			
			Twin	Full	Queen	King
△	light purple	T7	216	288	288	360
△	dark purple	T7	216	288	288	360
△	white	T7	432	576	576	720
		Totals	864	1,152	1,152	1,440

16″ block

Templates	Color	Code	Number of pieces needed for quilt			
			Twin	Full	Queen	King
△	light purple	T9	140	168	168	196
△	dark purple	T9	140	168	168	196
△	white	T9	280	336	336	392
		Totals	560	672	672	784

20″ block

Templates	Color	Code	Number of pieces needed for quilt			
			Twin	Full	Queen	King
△	light purple	T11	80	80	100	120
△	dark purple	T11	80	80	100	120
△	white	T11	160	160	200	240
		Totals	320	320	400	480

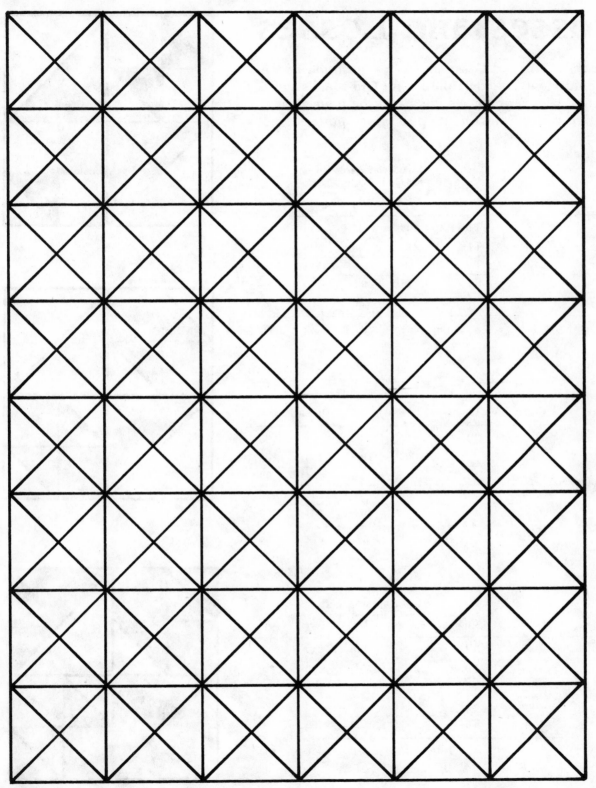

4-patch

Total pieces in block: 16

Crosses and Losses

Also named **Fox and Geese** and, with variation of the color placement, called **Triple X** and **Old Maid's Puzzle,** this design is another example of the hour glass motif that runs through many patchwork patterns.

12" block

Templates	Color	Code	Number of pieces needed for quilt			
			Twin	Full	Queen	King
△	blue	T10	108	144	144	180
△	black	T4	216	288	288	360
△	white	T10	108	144	144	180
☐	white	S3	216	288	288	360
△	white	T4	216	288	288	360
		Totals	864	1,152	1,152	1,440

16" block

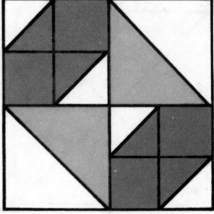

Templates	Color	Code	Number of pieces needed for quilt			
			Twin	Full	Queen	King
△	blue	T12*	70	84	84	98
△	black	T6	140	168	168	196
△	white	T12*	70	84	84	98
☐	white	S4	140	168	168	196
△	white	T6	140	168	168	196
		Totals	560	672	672	784

20" block

Templates	Color	Code	Number of pieces needed for quilt			
			Twin	Full	Queen	King
△	blue	T13*	40	40	50	60
△	black	T8	80	80	100	120
△	white	T13*	40	40	50	60
☐	white	S5	80	80	100	120
△	white	T8	80	80	100	120
		Totals	320	320	400	480

*Template outline not provided.

4-patch

Total pieces in block: 16

Sail Boat

Nautical themes were common in early patchwork designs, since most Americans could trace their family tree back to a sea-faring ancestor. Other design names which reflect this heritage are **Ocean Wave, Compass,** and **Storm-at-Sea.**

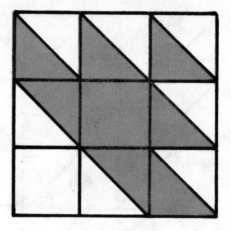

12″ block

Templates	Color	Code	Number of pieces needed for quilt			
			Twin	Full	Queen	King
△	purple	T6	378	504	504	630
☐	purple	S4	54	72	72	90
△	white	T6	378	504	504	630
☐	white	S4	54	72	72	90
		Totals	864	1,152	1,152	1,440

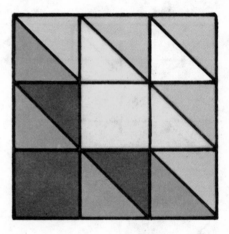

15″ block

Templates	Color	Code	Number of pieces needed for quilt			
			Twin	Full	Queen	King
△	purple	T8	245	294	294	392
☐	purple	S5	35	42	42	56
△	white	T8	245	294	294	392
☐	white	S5	35	42	42	56
		Totals	560	672	672	896

18″ block

Templates	Color	Code	Number of pieces needed for quilt			
			Twin	Full	Queen	King
△	purple	T10	168	210	210	252
☐	purple	S6	24	30	30	36
△	white	T10	168	210	210	252
☐	white	S6	24	30	30	36
		Totals	384	480	480	576

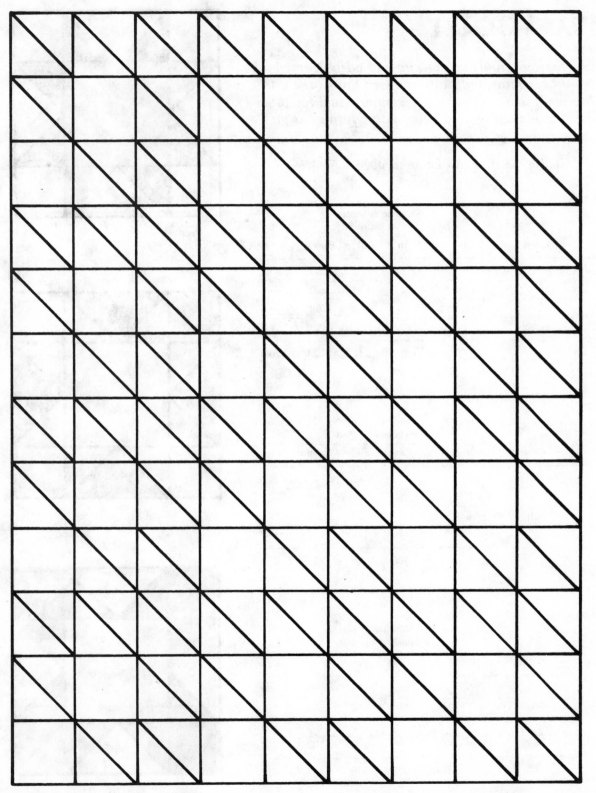

3-patch

Total pieces in block: 16

Saw Tooth

The saw was an important tool for the early farmer who cleared his land and built his own house with its help. The teeth of the saw suggested the name for this block design, as well as for a common overall design and for many border designs.

Also illustrated in **Latticework** chapter, page 155.

12" block

Templates	Color	Code	Number of pieces needed for quilt			
			Twin	Full	Queen	King
□	yellow	S6	54	72	72	90
△	green	T4	432	576	576	720
△	white	T7	216	288	288	360
□	white	S3	216	288	288	360
		Totals	918	1,224	1,224	1,530

16" block

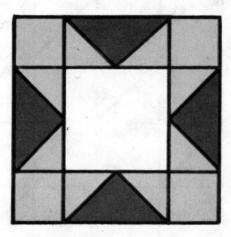

Templates	Color	Code	Number of pieces needed for quilt			
			Twin	Full	Queen	King
□	yellow	S7	35	42	42	49
△	green	T6	280	336	336	392
△	white	T9	140	168	168	196
□	white	S4	140	168	168	196
		Totals	595	714	714	833

20" block

Templates	Color	Code	Number of pieces needed for quilt			
			Twin	Full	Queen	King
□	yellow	S8	20	20	25	30
△	green	T8	160	160	200	240
△	white	T11	80	80	100	120
□	white	S5	80	80	100	120
		Totals	340	340	425	510

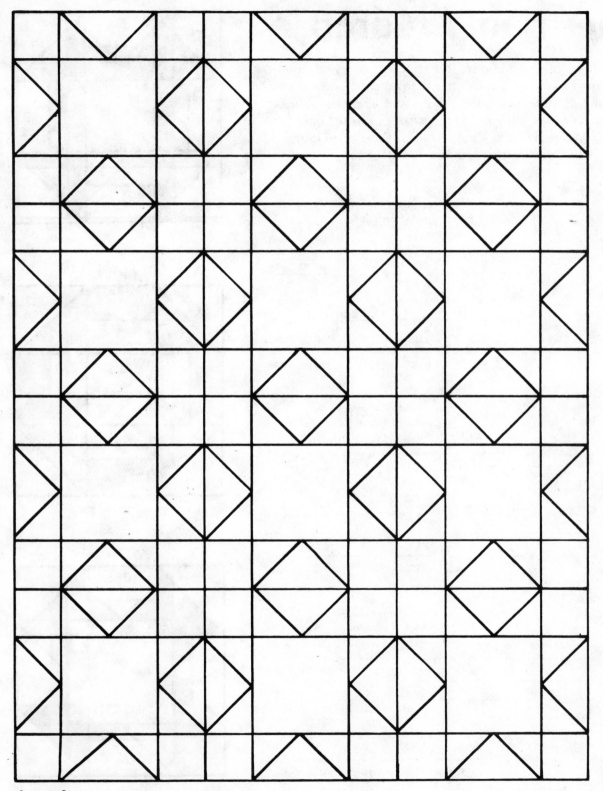

4-patch

Total pieces in block: 17

Sherman's March

*A variation of the basic **Nine-Patch,** this design commemorates General Sherman's "March to the Sea" through Georgia during the Civil War. The design also has other names with more pleasant connotations:* **Monkey Wrench, Love-Knot, Hole-in-the-Barn-Door, Puss-in-the-Corner,** *and* **Lincoln's Platform.**

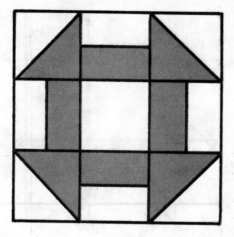

12″ block

Templates	Color	Code	Number of pieces needed for quilt			
			Twin	Full	Queen	King
△	green	T6	216	288	288	360
▭	green	R1	216	288	288	360
△	white	T6	216	288	288	360
▢	white	S4	54	72	72	90
▭	white	R1	216	288	288	360
		Totals	918	1,224	1,224	1,530

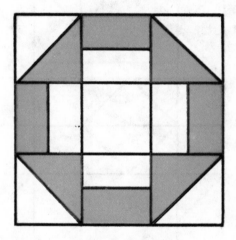

15″ block

Templates	Color	Code	Number of pieces needed for quilt			
			Twin	Full	Queen	King
△	green	T8	140	168	168	224
▭	green	R2	140	168	168	224
△	white	T8	140	168	168	224
▢	white	S5	35	42	42	56
▭	white	R2	140	168	168	224
		Totals	595	714	714	952

18″ block

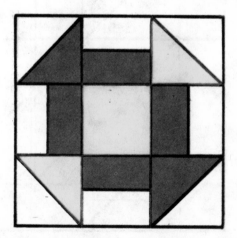

Templates	Color	Code	Number of pieces needed for quilt			
			Twin	Full	Queen	King
△	green	T10	96	120	120	144
▭	green	R3	96	120	120	144
△	white	T10	96	120	120	144
▢	white	S6	24	30	30	36
▭	white	R3	96	120	120	144
		Totals	408	510	510	612

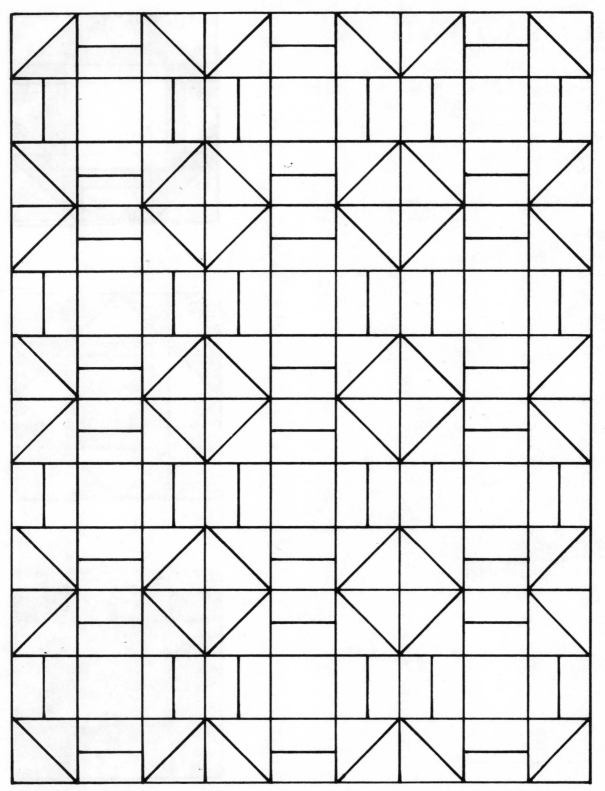

3-patch

Total pieces in block: 17

King's Crown

No one knows whether this design was named after King George of England or King David of the Bible. The quiltmaker's opinion on the matter probably depended on whether earthly or heavenly matters were more pressing when the quilt top was pieced.

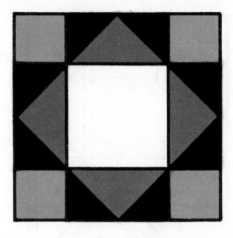

12″ block

Templates	Color	Code	Number of pieces needed for quilt			
			Twin	Full	Queen	King
□	white	S6	54	72	72	90
△	blue	T7	216	288	288	360
△	black	T4	432	576	576	720
□	green	S3	216	288	288	360
		Totals	918	1,224	1,224	1,530

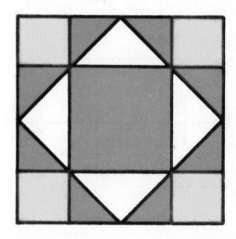

16″ block

Templates	Color	Code	Number of pieces needed for quilt			
			Twin	Full	Queen	King
□	white	S7	35	42	42	49
△	blue	T9	140	168	168	196
△	black	T6	280	336	336	392
□	green	S4	140	168	168	196
		Totals	595	714	714	833

20″ block

Templates	Color	Code	Number of pieces needed for quilt			
			Twin	Full	Queen	King
□	white	S8	20	20	25	30
△	blue	T11	80	80	100	120
△	black	T8	160	160	200	240
□	green	S5	80	80	100	120
		Totals	340	340	425	510

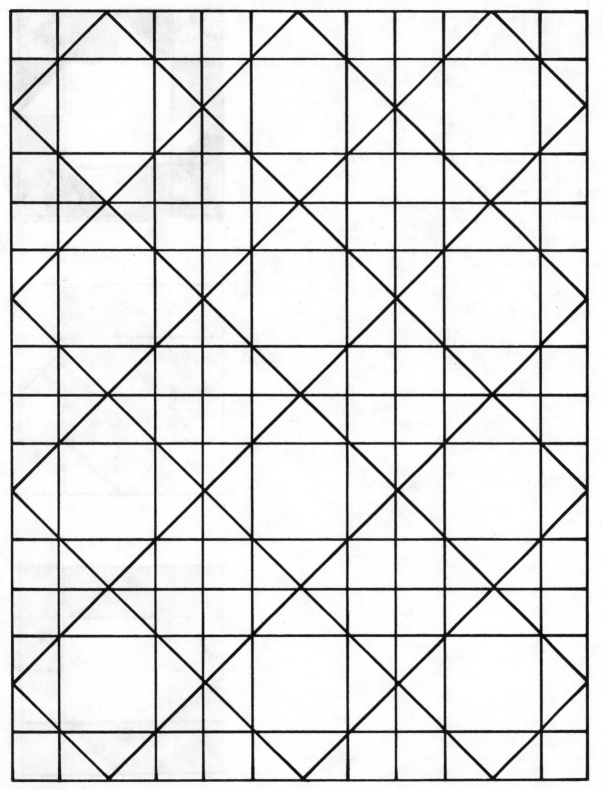

4-patch

Total pieces in block: 17

Pin-Wheel

A breath of air sends the pin-wheel whirling, its colors merging in rainbow brilliance. This design depicts a child's pin-wheel, yet it has other names as well: **Sugar Bowl, Fly, Kathy's Ramble, Crow's Foot, Fan Mill,** *and* **Flutter Wheels.**

Also illustrated in **Latticework** *chapter, page 160.*

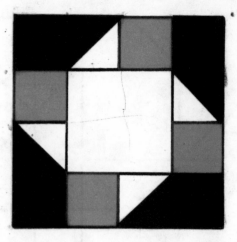

12″ block

Templates	Color	Code	Number of pieces needed for quilt			
			Twin	Full	Queen	King
□	white	S6	54	72	72	90
△	white	T4	216	288	288	360
□	red	S3	216	288	288	360
□	black	S3	216	288	288	360
△	black	T4	216	288	288	360
		Totals	918	1,224	1,224	1,530

16″ block

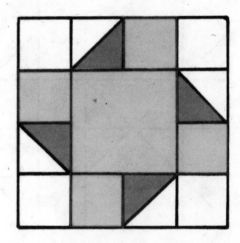

Templates	Color	Code	Number of pieces needed for quilt			
			Twin	Full	Queen	King
□	white	S7	35	42	42	49
△	white	T6	140	168	168	196
□	red	S4	140	168	168	196
□	black	S4	140	168	168	196
△	black	T6	140	168	168	196
		Totals	595	714	714	833

(336)

20″ block

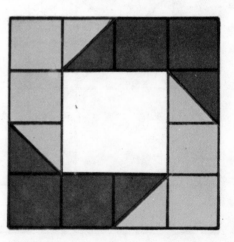

Templates	Color	Code	Number of pieces needed for quilt			
			Twin	Full	Queen	King
□	white	S8	20	20	25	30
△	white	T8	80	80	100	120
□	red	S5	80	80	100	120
□	black	S5	80	80	100	120
△	black	T8	80	80	100	120
		Totals	340	340	425	510

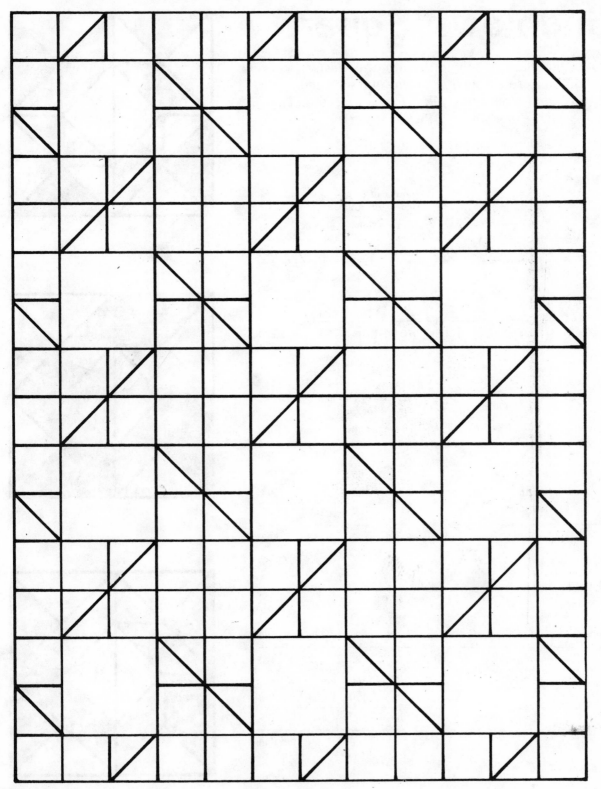

4-patch

Total pieces in block: 17

Windblown Square

With its suggestion of rolling motion, this design probably reminded prairie women of the tumbleweeds which the wind blew willy-nilly across the land. This pattern is also called **Balkan Puzzle**.

Also illustrated in **Latticework** chapter, page 154.

12" block

Templates	Color	Code	Number of pieces needed for quilt			
			Twin	Full	Queen	King
△	green	T7	216	288	288	360
▱	blue	P1	216	288	288	360
△	white	T7	324	432	432	540
△	white	T4	216	288	288	360
		Totals	972	1,296	1,296	1,620

16" block

Templates	Color	Code	Number of pieces needed for quilt			
			Twin	Full	Queen	King
△	green	T9	140	168	168	196
▱	blue	P2	140	168	168	196
△	white	T9	210	252	252	294
△	white	T6	140	168	168	196
		Totals	630	756	756	882

20" block

Templates	Color	Code	Number of pieces needed for quilt			
			Twin	Full	Queen	King
△	green	T11	80	80	100	120
▱	blue	P3*	80	80	100	120
△	white	T11	120	120	150	180
△	white	T8	80	80	100	120
		Totals	360	360	450	540

*Template outline not provided.

4-patch

Total pieces in block: 18

Odd Fellows' Cross

One of the numerous patterns named for a religious symbol, this design reflects the deep and abiding religious faith of many quiltmakers. Other patterns with names having religious significance are **Tree Everlasting, Crown-of-Thorns,** *and* **Cross-Upon-Cross.**

12″ block

Templates	Color	Code	Number of pieces needed for quilt			
			Twin	Full	Queen	King
△	gray	T7	108	144	144	180
△	pink	T7	216	288	288	360
△	pink	T4	216	288	288	360
△	white	T7	216	288	288	360
□	white	S3	216	288	288	360
		Totals	972	1,296	1,296	1,620

16″ block

Templates	Color	Code	Number of pieces needed for quilt			
			Twin	Full	Queen	King
△	gray	T9	70	84	84	98
△	pink	T9	140	168	168	196
△	pink	T6	140	168	168	196
△	white	T9	140	168	168	196
□	white	S4	140	168	168	196
		Totals	630	756	756	882

20″ block

Templates	Color	Code	Number of pieces needed for quilt			
			Twin	Full	Queen	King
△	gray	T11	40	40	50	60
△	pink	T11	80	80	100	120
△	pink	T8	80	80	100	120
△	white	T11	80	80	100	120
□	white	S5	80	80	100	120
		Totals	360	360	450	540

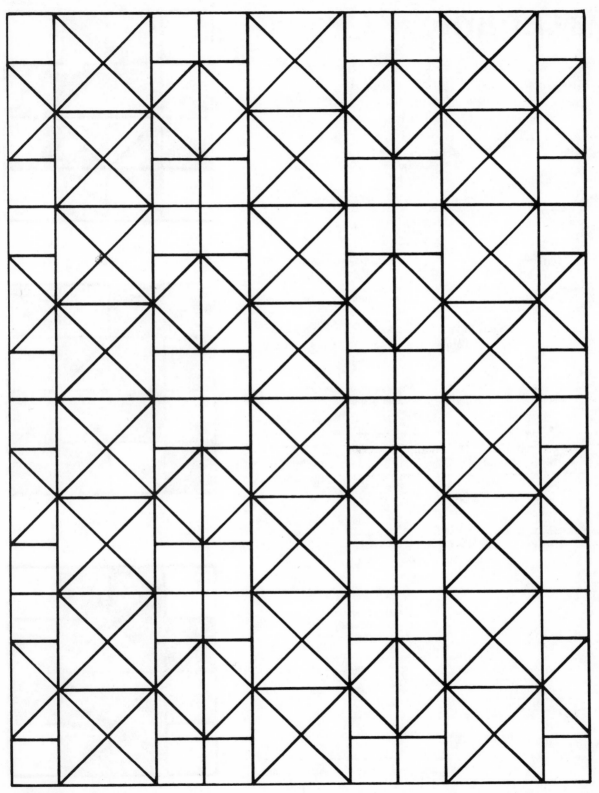

4-patch

Total pieces in block: 18

Susannah

We like to think that this design was inspired by that old Stephen Foster song "Oh, Susanna." It has even been suggested that the center of the block resembles the banjo mentioned in the refrain.

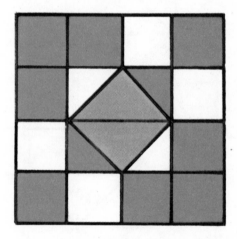

12" block

Templates	Color	Code	Number of pieces needed for quilt			
			Twin	Full	Queen	King
☐	orange	S3	216	288	288	360
△	orange	T4	216	288	288	360
☐	yellow	S3	216	288	288	360
☐	white	S3	216	288	288	360
△	white	T7	108	144	144	180
		Totals	972	1,296	1,296	1,620

16" block

Templates	Color	Code	Number of pieces needed for quilt			
			Twin	Full	Queen	King
☐	orange	S4	140	168	168	196
△	orange	T6	140	168	168	196
☐	yellow	S4	140	168	168	196
☐	white	S4	140	168	168	196
△	white	T9	70	84	84	98
		Totals	630	756	756	882

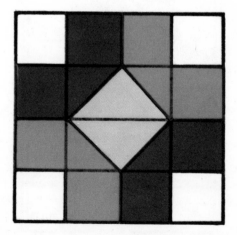

20" block

Templates	Color	Code	Number of pieces needed for quilt			
			Twin	Full	Queen	King
☐	orange	S5	80	80	100	120
△	orange	T8	80	80	100	120
☐	yellow	S5	80	80	100	120
☐	white	S5	80	80	100	120
△	white	T11	40	40	50	60
		Totals	360	360	450	540

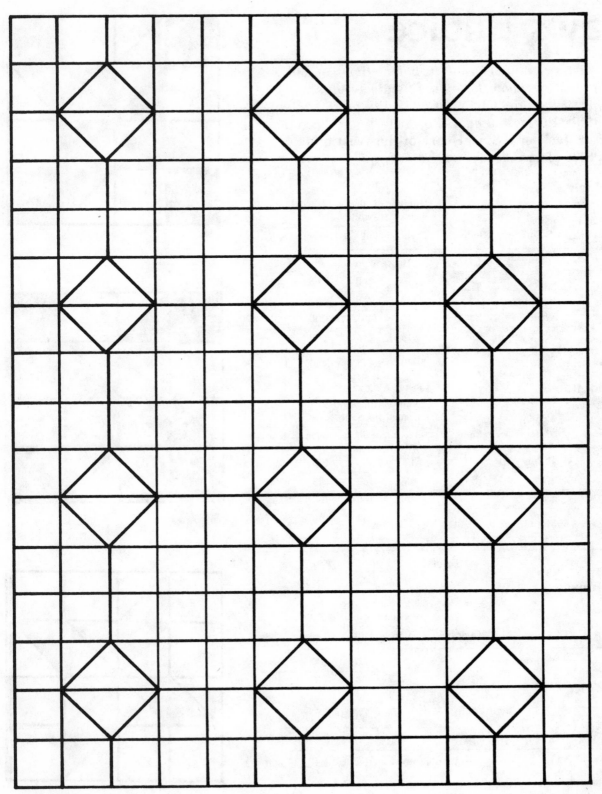

4-patch

Total pieces in block: 18

Clay's Choice

This design originated in the turbulent times of Calhoun and Clay, when the issue of states' rights was the topic of the day. **CLAY'S CHOICE** was re-named many times during the course of history and became known as **Jackson's Star, Henry-of-the-West** and finally **Star-of-the-West.**

12″ block

Templates	Color	Code	Number of pieces needed for quilt			
			Twin	Full	Queen	King
▱	yellow	P1	216	288	288	360
▢	gray	S3	216	288	288	360
△	gray	T4	216	288	288	360
▢	white	S3	216	288	288	360
△	white	T4	216	288	288	360
		Totals	**1,080**	**1,440**	**1,440**	**1,800**

16″ block

Templates	Color	Code	Number of pieces needed for quilt			
			Twin	Full	Queen	King
▱	yellow	P2	140	168	168	196
▢	gray	S4	140	168	168	196
△	gray	T6	140	168	168	196
▢	white	S4	140	168	168	196
△	white	T6	140	168	168	196
		Totals	**700**	**840**	**840**	**980**

20″ block

Templates	Color	Code	Number of pieces needed for quilt			
			Twin	Full	Queen	King
▱	yellow	P3*	80	80	100	120
▢	gray	S5	80	80	100	120
△	gray	T8	80	80	100	120
▢	white	S5	80	80	100	120
△	white	T8	80	80	100	120
		Totals	**400**	**400**	**500**	**600**

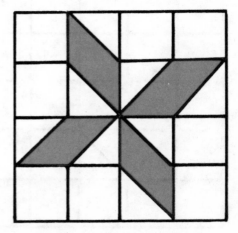

*Template outline not provided.

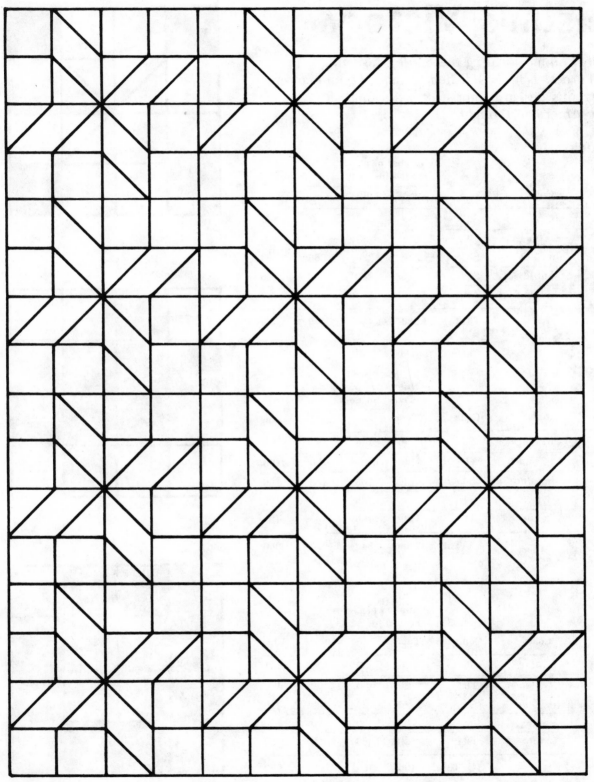

4-patch

Total pieces in block: 20

Nelson's Victory

Probably commemorating the battle of Trafalgar in which Lord Nelson established British dominance on the seas, this design demonstrates the English influence in early American thought.

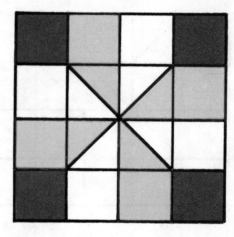

12″ block

Templates	Color	Code	Number of pieces needed for quilt			
			Twin	Full	Queen	King
□	lt. blue	S3	216	288	288	360
△	lt. blue	T4	216	288	288	360
□	dk. blue	S3	216	288	288	360
□	white	S3	216	288	288	360
△	white	T4	216	288	288	360
		Totals	**1,080**	**1,440**	**1,440**	**1,800**

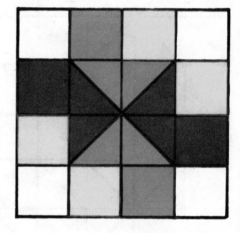

16″ block

Templates	Color	Code	Number of pieces needed for quilt			
			Twin	Full	Queen	King
□	lt. blue	S4	140	168	168	196
△	lt. blue	T6	140	168	168	196
□	dk. blue	S4	140	168	168	196
□	white	S4	140	168	168	196
△	white	T6	140	168	168	196
		Totals	**700**	**840**	**840**	**980**

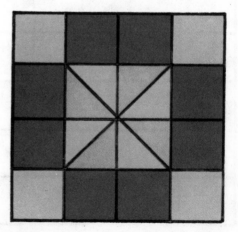

20″ block

Templates	Color	Code	Number of pieces needed for quilt			
			Twin	Full	Queen	King
□	lt. blue	S5	80	80	100	120
△	lt. blue	T8	80	80	100	120
□	dk. blue	S5	80	80	100	120
□	white	S5	80	80	100	120
△	white	T8	80	80	100	120
		Totals	**400**	**400**	**500**	**600**

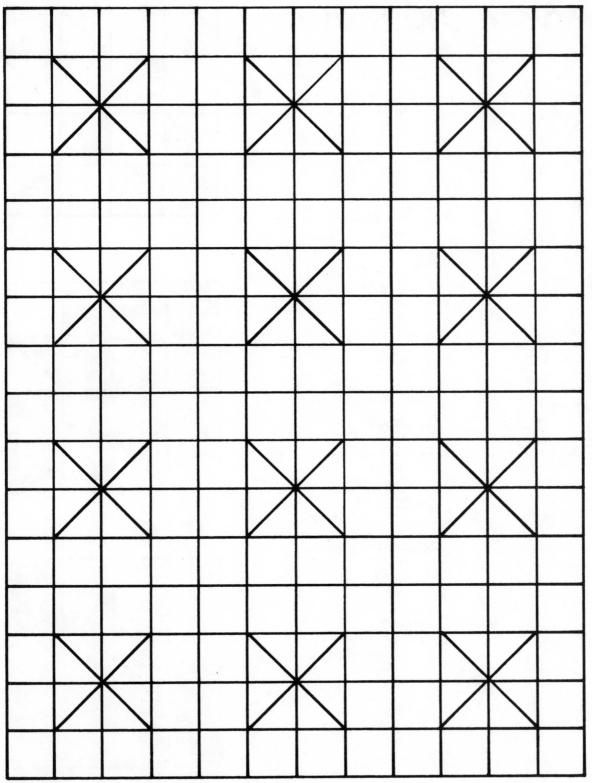

4-patch

Total pieces in block: 20

Road-to-Oklahoma

A variation of **Jacob's Ladder** *and* **Road-to-California** *and also called* **New Four-Patch,** *this design memorializes another facet of pioneer life—the hardships encountered in crossing the frontier to begin a new life in the West.*

Also illustrated in the **Latticework** *chapter, page 156, and in the* **Rotated Block** *chapter, page 168.*

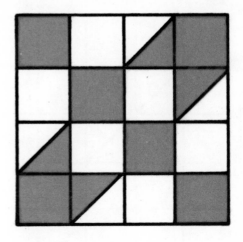

12″ block

Templates	Color	Code	Number of pieces needed for quilt			
			Twin	Full	Queen	King
△	red	T4	216	288	288	360
□	red	S3	324	432	432	540
△	white	T4	216	288	288	360
□	white	S3	324	432	432	540
		Totals	1,080	1,440	1,440	1,800

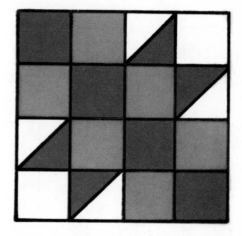

16″ block

Templates	Color	Code	Number of pieces needed for quilt			
			Twin	Full	Queen	King
△	red	T6	140	168	168	196
□	red	S4	210	252	252	294
△	white	T6	140	168	168	196
□	white	S4	210	252	252	294
		Totals	700	840	840	980

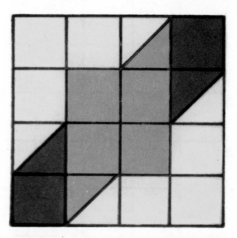

20″ block

Templates	Color	Code	Number of pieces needed for quilt			
			Twin	Full	Queen	King
△	red	T8	80	80	100	120
□	red	S5	120	120	150	180
△	white	T8	80	80	100	120
□	white	S5	120	120	150	180
		Totals	400	400	500	600

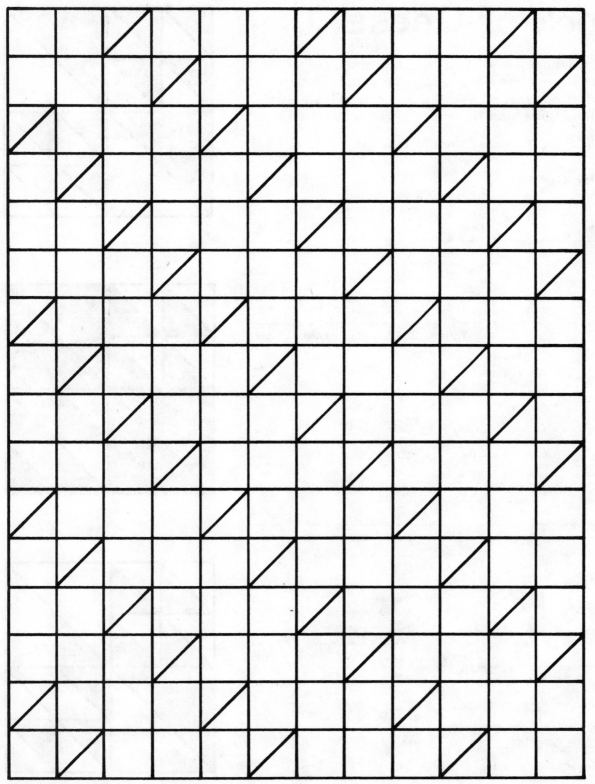

4-patch

Total pieces in block: 20

Flock-of-Geese

An old colonial pattern, this design brings to mind the flight of white geese winging together against a blue sky. Other patterns born of this scene are **Flying Swallows, Blue Birds,** *and* **Hovering Hawks** *(page 104).*

Also illustrated in **Rotated Block** *chapter, page 167.*

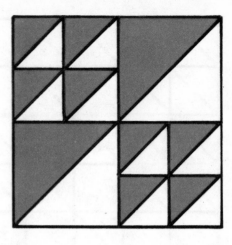

12″ block

Templates	Color	Code	Number of pieces needed for quilt			
			Twin	Full	Queen	King
△	blue	T4	432	576	576	720
△	blue	T10	108	144	144	180
△	white	T4	432	576	576	720
△	white	T10	108	144	144	180
		Totals	1,080	1,440	1,440	1,800

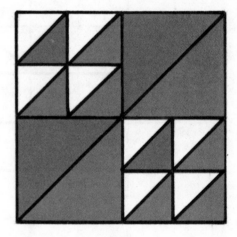

16″ block

Templates	Color	Code	Number of pieces needed for quilt			
			Twin	Full	Queen	King
△	blue	T6	280	336	336	392
△	blue	T12*	70	84	84	98
△	white	T6	280	336	336	392
△	white	T12*	70	84	84	98
		Totals	700	840	840	980

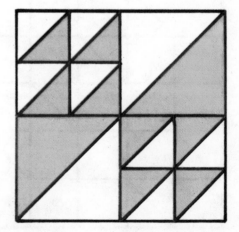

20″ block

Templates	Color	Code	Number of pieces needed for quilt			
			Twin	Full	Queen	King
△	blue	T8	160	160	200	240
△	blue	T13*	40	40	50	60
△	white	T8	160	160	200	240
△	white	T13*	40	40	50	60
		Totals	400	400	500	600

*Template outline not provided.

4-patch

Total pieces in block: 20

Texas Star

Every state has had at least one patchwork pattern named for it, and this is Texas'. When pieced in two colors its name becomes **Ohio Star.** *Other names for this pattern are* **Variable Star** *and* **Lone Star.**

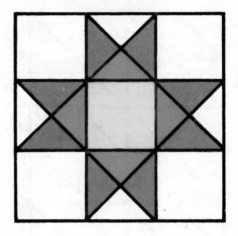

12" block

Templates	Color	Code	Number of pieces needed for quilt			
			Twin	Full	Queen	King
☐	yellow	S4	54	72	72	90
△	red	T3	216	288	288	360
△	blue	T3	432	576	576	720
☐	white	S4	216	288	288	360
△	white	T3	216	288	288	360
		Totals	1,134	1,512	1,512	1,890

15" block

Templates	Color	Code	Number of pieces needed for quilt			
			Twin	Full	Queen	King
☐	yellow	S5	35	42	42	56
△	red	T5	140	168	168	224
△	blue	T5	280	336	336	448
☐	white	S5	140	168	168	224
△	white	T5	140	168	168	224
		Totals	735	882	882	1,176

18" block

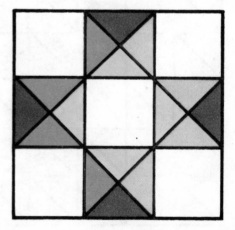

Templates	Color	Code	Number of pieces needed for quilt			
			Twin	Full	Queen	King
☐	yellow	S6	24	30	30	36
△	red	T7	96	120	120	144
△	blue	T7	192	240	240	288
☐	white	S6	96	120	120	144
△	white	T7	96	120	120	144
		Totals	504	630	630	756

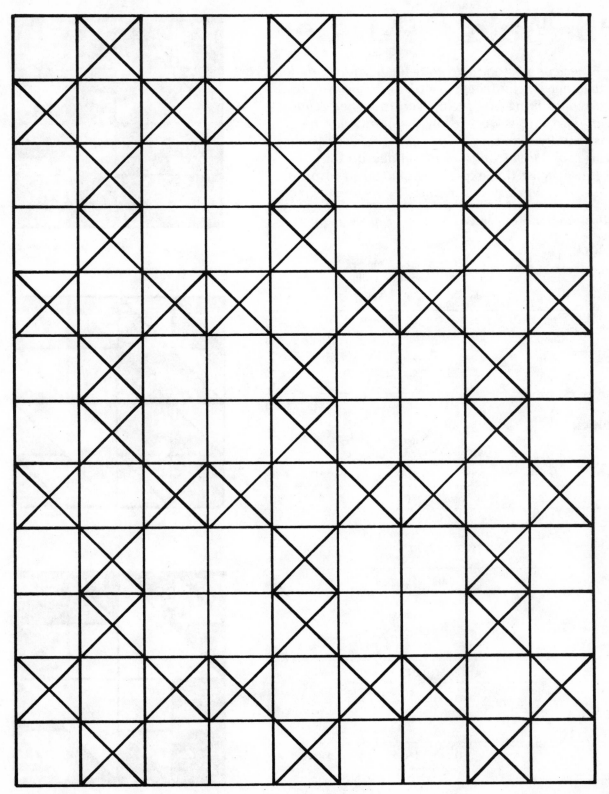

3-patch
Total pieces in block: 21

Old Maid's Puzzle

Early American custom held that for a young girl to piece together her marriage quilt before she was betrothed would bring bad luck. Even after her engagement, the girl rarely worked on her own wedding quilt. Friends usually made it for her as a gift. Woe to the girl who broke this tradition and ended up an old maid! But at least this experience lent itself to an interesting patchwork design name.

Also illustrated in **Rotated Block** chapter, page 166.

12" block

Templates	Color	Code	Number of pieces needed for quilt			
			Twin	Full	Queen	King
△	blue	T4	540	720	720	900
□	blue	S3	216	288	288	360
△	red	T4	324	432	432	540
△	red	T10	108	144	144	180
		Totals	**1,188**	**1,584**	**1,584**	**1,980**

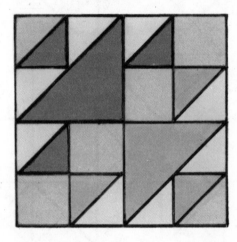

16" block

Templates	Color	Code	Number of pieces needed for quilt			
			Twin	Full	Queen	King
△	blue	T6	350	420	420	490
□	blue	S4	140	168	168	196
△	red	T6	210	252	252	294
△	red	T12*	70	84	84	98
		Totals	**770**	**924**	**924**	**1,078**

20" block

Templates	Color	Code	Number of pieces needed for quilt			
			Twin	Full	Queen	King
△	blue	T8	200	200	250	300
□	blue	S5	80	80	100	120
△	red	T8	120	120	150	180
△	red	T13*	40	40	50	60
		Totals	**440**	**440**	**550**	**660**

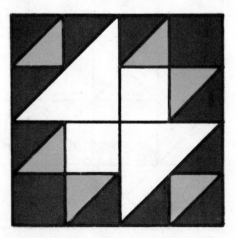

*Template outline not provided.

4-patch

Total pieces in block: 22

Hovering Hawks

Hawks can swoop down and carry away small domestic farm animals like chickens, as well as pests like rats and mice. Therefore, the **Hovering Hawks** *represented by this pattern were not a welcome sight at pioneer farms.*

Also illustrated in **Rotated Block** *chapter, page 170.*

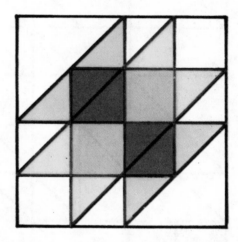

12″ block

Templates	Color	Code	Number of pieces needed for quilt			
			Twin	Full	Queen	King
△	white	T4	540	720	720	900
△	green	T4	324	432	432	540
□	green	S3	216	288	288	360
△	green	T10	108	144	144	180
		Totals	1,188	1,584	1,584	1,980

16″ block

Templates	Color	Code	Number of pieces needed for quilt			
			Twin	Full	Queen	King
△	white	T6	350	420	420	490
△	green	T6	210	252	252	294
□	green	S4	140	168	168	196
△	green	T12*	70	84	84	98
		Totals	770	924	924	1,078

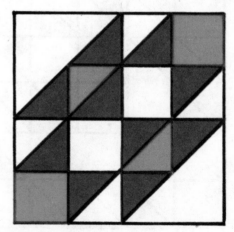

20″ block

Templates	Color	Code	Number of pieces needed for quilt			
			Twin	Full	Queen	King
△	white	T8	200	200	250	300
△	green	T8	120	120	150	180
□	green	S5	80	80	100	120
△	green	T13*	40	40	50	60
		Totals	440	440	550	660

*Template outline not provided.

4-patch

Total pieces in block: 22

What-You-Will

As best we can determine, this versatile design has come down through the years without ever having been given a name that firmly stuck! Many of the designs in this chapter have alternate names. This pattern . . . call it what-you-will.

12″ block

Templates	Color	Code	Number of pieces needed for quilt			
			Twin	Full	Queen	King
▱	brown	P1	216	288	288	360
▱	yellow	P1	216	288	288	360
△	brown	T4	432	576	576	720
△	yellow	T4	432	576	576	720
		Totals	1,296	1,728	1,728	2,160

16″ block

Templates	Color	Code	Number of pieces needed for quilt			
			Twin	Full	Queen	King
▱	brown	P2	140	168	168	196
▱	yellow	P2	140	168	168	196
△	brown	T6	280	336	336	392
△	yellow	T6	280	336	336	392
		Totals	840	1,008	1,008	1,176

20″ block

Templates	Color	Code	Number of pieces needed for quilt			
			Twin	Full	Queen	King
▱	brown	P3*	80	80	100	120
▱	yellow	P3*	80	80	100	120
△	brown	T8	160	160	200	240
△	yellow	T8	160	160	200	240
		Totals	480	480	600	720

*Template outline not provided.

3-patch

Total pieces in block: 24

Columns

Many old patchwork designs look very much like modern art. **Columns** is an example of a simple star-like design which, through careful placement of color, creates an optical illusion of great visual depth.

Note: This design requires that the template for the parallelogram be inverted when tracing one-half of the patches.

12" block

Templates	Color	Code	Number of pieces needed for quilt			
			Twin	Full	Queen	King
▱	green	P1	216	288	288	360
▱	light orange	P1	216	288	288	360
△	dark orange	T4	432	576	576	720
△	white	T4	432	576	576	720
		Totals	**1,296**	**1,728**	**1,728**	**2,160**

16" block

Templates	Color	Code	Number of pieces needed for quilt			
			Twin	Full	Queen	King
▱	green	P2	140	168	168	196
▱	light orange	P2	140	168	168	196
△	dark orange	T6	280	336	336	392
△	white	T6	280	336	336	392
		Totals	**840**	**1,008**	**1,008**	**1,176**

20" block

Templates	Color	Code	Number of pieces needed for quilt			
			Twin	Full	Queen	King
▱	green	P3*	80	80	100	120
▱	light orange	P3*	80	80	100	120
△	dark orange	T8	160	160	200	240
△	white	T8	160	160	200	240
		Totals	**480**	**480**	**600**	**720**

*Template outline not provided.

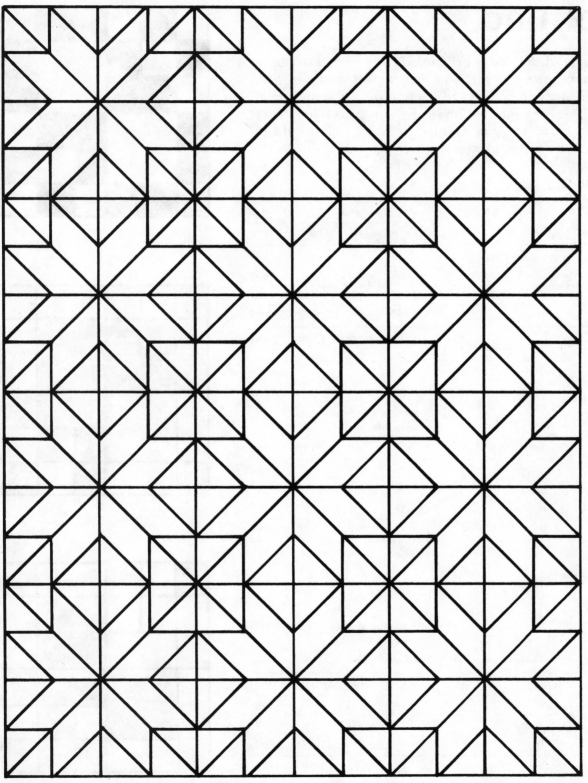

4-patch

Total pieces in block: 24

Domino

The game of dominoes originated in the Far East but became a popular American amusement in the eighteenth century. A whimsical version of this design, which gives the impression of domino pieces laid next to each other, could be created by using polka-dot fabric for some of the pieces.

12″ block

Templates	Color	Code	Number of pieces needed for quilt			
			Twin	Full	Queen	King
▭	black	R1	324	432	432	540
▭	black	S1	324	432	432	540
▭	white	S4	108	144	144	180
▭	white	S1	540	720	720	900
		Totals	**1,296**	**1,728**	**1,728**	**2,160**

15″ block

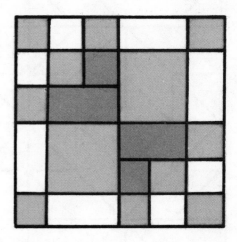

Templates	Color	Code	Number of pieces needed for quilt			
			Twin	Full	Queen	King
▭	black	R2	210	252	252	336
▭	black	S2	210	252	252	336
▭	white	S5	70	84	84	112
▭	white	S2	350	420	420	560
		Totals	**840**	**1,008**	**1,008**	**1,344**

18″ block

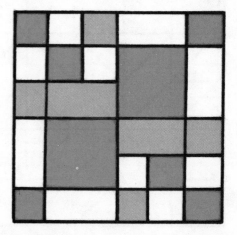

Templates	Color	Code	Number of pieces needed for quilt			
			Twin	Full	Queen	King
▭	black	R3	144	180	180	216
▭	black	S3	144	180	180	216
▭	white	S6	48	60	60	72
▭	white	S3	240	300	300	360
		Totals	**576**	**720**	**720**	**864**

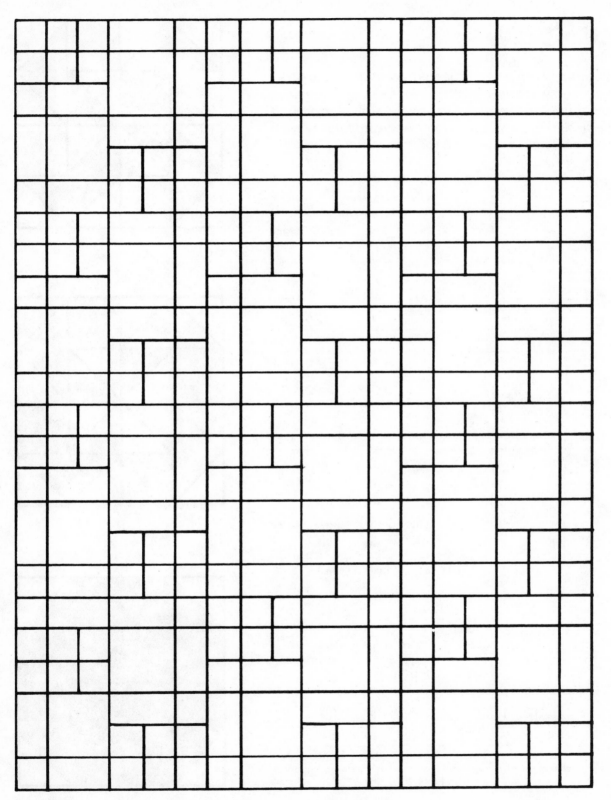

3-patch

Total pieces in block: 24

See-Saw

One plaything which is fairly easy to make for children and brings them hours of enjoyment is a see-saw or teeter-totter—one narrow board over a fulcrum will do. The design in this block appears to include two see-saws, crossing in the center.

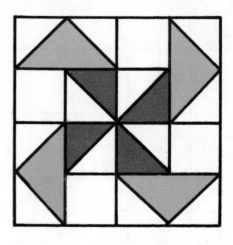

12″ block

Templates	Color	Code	Number of pieces needed for quilt			
			Twin	Full	Queen	King
△	light purple	T7	216	288	288	360
△	dark purple	T4	216	288	288	360
□	white	S3	216	288	288	360
△	white	T4	648	864	864	1,080
		Totals	1,296	1,728	1,728	2,160

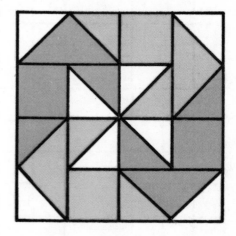

16″ block

Templates	Color	Code	Number of pieces needed for quilt			
			Twin	Full	Queen	King
△	light purple	T9	140	168	168	196
△	dark purple	T6	140	168	168	196
□	white	S4	140	168	168	196
△	white	T6	420	504	504	588
		Totals	840	1,008	1,008	1,176

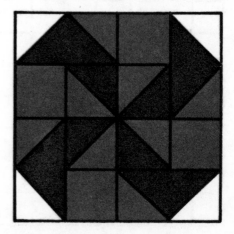

20″ block

Templates	Color	Code	Number of pieces needed for quilt			
			Twin	Full	Queen	King
△	light purple	T11	80	80	100	120
△	dark purple	T8	80	80	100	120
□	white	S5	80	80	100	120
△	white	T8	240	240	300	360
		Totals	480	480	600	720

4-patch

Total pieces in block: 24

Letter X

Most pioneer women were responsible for educating their children as well as feeding, clothing, and otherwise caring for their families. Thus it is not surprising that the alphabet was a popular source of patchwork design names since teaching their children to read was a daily activity. Other patterns named for letters are **Double X, X-Quisite, Double Z,** and **Madame X.**

12″ block

Templates	Color	Code	Number of pieces needed for quilt			
			Twin	Full	Queen	King
□	blue	S4	216	288	288	360
△	blue	T3	540	720	720	900
△	white	T3	540	720	720	900
		Totals	1,296	1,728	1,728	2,160

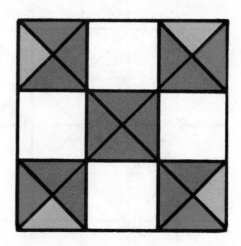

15″ block

Templates	Color	Code	Number of pieces needed for quilt			
			Twin	Full	Queen	King
□	blue	S5	140	168	168	224
△	blue	T5	350	420	420	560
△	white	T5	350	420	420	560
		Totals	840	1,008	1,008	1,344

18″ block

Templates	Color	Code	Number of pieces needed for quilt			
			Twin	Full	Queen	King
□	blue	S6	96	120	120	144
△	blue	T7	240	300	300	360
△	white	T7	240	300	300	360
		Totals	576	720	720	864

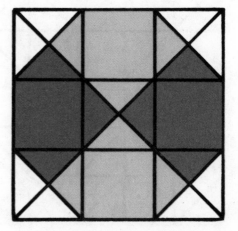

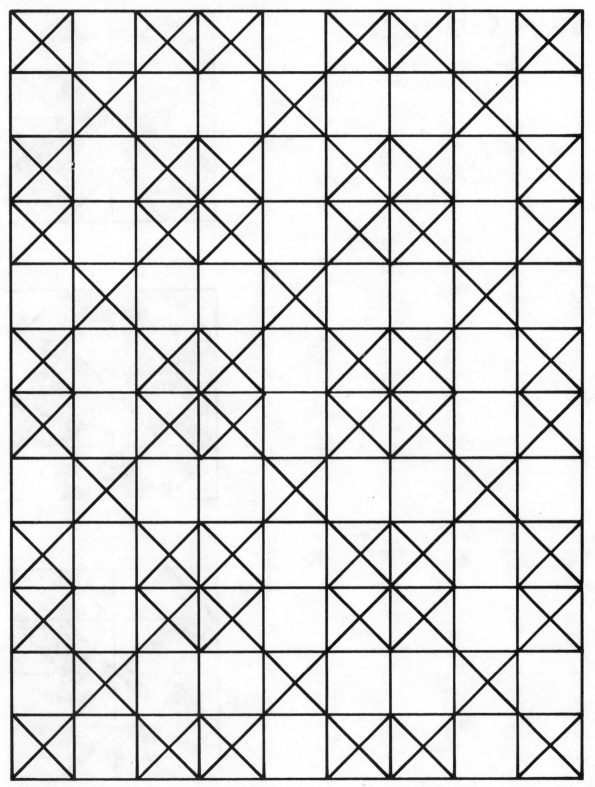

3-patch

Total pieces in block: 24

Brown Goose

Geese were a familiar sight on farms, since they were raised to provide the feathers needed for filling comforters and pillows. This pattern was a familiar sight as well, popular because it is easy to piece and its traditional brown colors do not show dirt, making it an easy quilt to care for.

Also illustrated in **Rotated Block** chapter, page 174.

12" block

Templates	Color	Code	Number of pieces needed for quilt			
			Twin	Full	Queen	King
△	light brown	T7	216	288	288	360
▱	dark brown	P1	216	288	288	360
△	white	T4	864	1,152	1,152	1,440
		Totals	1,296	1,728	1,728	2,160

16" block

Templates	Color	Code	Number of pieces needed for quilt			
			Twin	Full	Queen	King
△	light brown	T9	140	168	168	196
▱	dark brown	P2	140	168	168	196
△	white	T6	560	672	672	784
		Totals	840	1,008	1,008	1,176

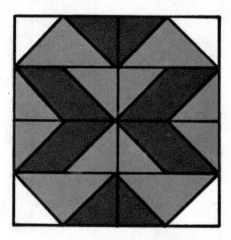

20" block

Templates	Color	Code	Number of pieces needed for quilt			
			Twin	Full	Queen	King
△	light brown	T11	80	80	100	120
▱	dark brown	P3*	80	80	100	120
△	white	T8	320	320	400	480
		Totals	480	480	600	720

*Template outline not provided.

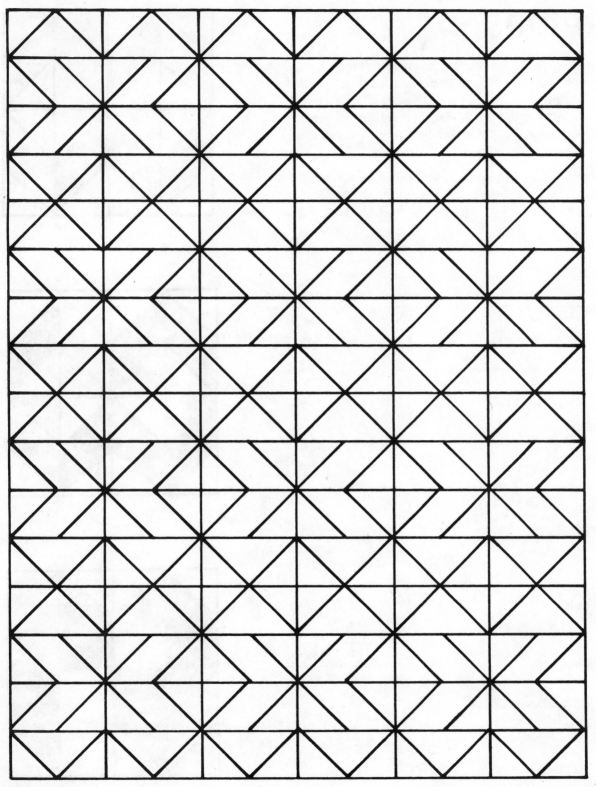

4-patch

Total pieces in block: 24

Ribbons

This configuration is one of the oldest forms known to the decorative arts. While usually representing the motion of water, here it resembles two ribbons twisting across a patchwork quilt. An interesting three dimensional effect can be achieved by using a monochromatic color scheme.

Also illustrated in **Rotated Block** *chapter, page 169.*
Note: This design requires that the template for the parallelogram be inverted when tracing one-half of the patches.

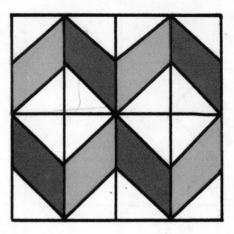

12" block

Templates	Color	Code	Number of pieces needed for quilt			
			Twin	Full	Queen	King
▱	pink	P1	216	288	288	360
▱	purple	P1	216	288	288	360
△	white	T4	864	1,152	1,152	1,440
		Totals	1,296	1,728	1,728	2,160

16" block

Templates	Color	Code	Number of pieces needed for quilt			
			Twin	Full	Queen	King
▱	pink	P2	140	168	168	196
▱	purple	P2	140	168	168	196
△	white	T6	560	672	672	784
		Totals	840	1,008	1,008	1,176

20" block

Templates	Color	Code	Number of pieces needed for quilt			
			Twin	Full	Queen	King
▱	pink	P3*	80	80	100	120
▱	purple	P3*	80	80	100	120
△	white	T8	320	320	400	480
		Totals	480	480	600	720

*Template outline not provided.

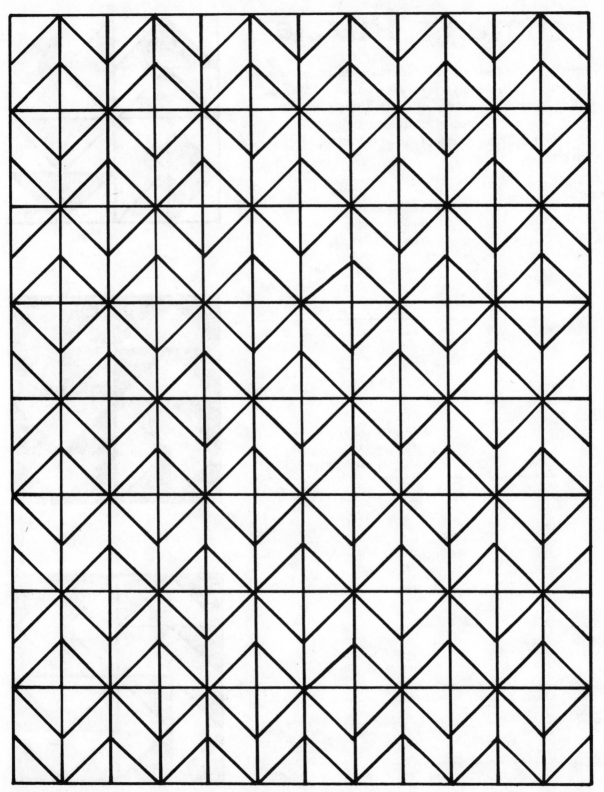

4-patch

Total pieces in block: 24

Dutchman's Puzzle

An adaptation of **Windmill,** this design was popular in the early 1800's. It probably received its name because it reminded Dutch immigrants of their homeland. Puzzles were a popular theme for quilt designs, some common ones being **Balkan Puzzle, Chinese Puzzle,** and **Devil's Puzzle.**

12" block

Templates	Color	Code	Number of pieces needed for quilt			
			Twin	Full	Queen	King
△	blue	T7	216	288	288	360
△	yellow	T7	216	288	288	360
△	white	T4	864	1,152	1,152	1,440
		Totals	1,296	1,728	1,728	2,160

16" block

Templates	Color	Code	Number of pieces needed for quilt			
			Twin	Full	Queen	King
△	blue	T9	140	168	168	196
△	yellow	T9	140	168	168	196
△	white	T6	560	672	672	784
		Totals	840	1,008	1,008	1,176

20" block

Templates	Color	Code	Number of pieces needed for quilt			
			Twin	Full	Queen	King
△	blue	T11	80	80	100	120
△	yellow	T11	80	80	100	120
△	white	T8	320	320	400	480
		Totals	480	480	600	720

4-patch

Total pieces in block: 24

Next-Door Neighbor

The great distance between pioneer farms and the nearest town prevented frequent visits. Thus, the next-door neighbors were important, both for their social visits and for their possible help in an emergency.

12" block

Templates	Color	Code	Number of pieces needed for quilt			
			Twin	Full	Queen	King
△	red	T7	108	144	144	180
△	red	T4	108	144	144	180
△	brown	T7	108	144	144	180
△	brown	T4	108	144	144	180
△	white	T7	216	288	288	360
△	white	T4	648	864	864	1,080
		Totals	1,296	1,728	1,728	2,160

16" block

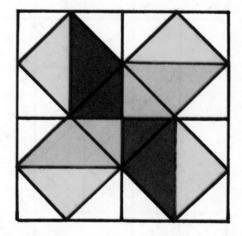

Templates	Color	Code	Number of pieces needed for quilt			
			Twin	Full	Queen	King
△	red	T9	70	84	84	98
△	red	T6	70	84	84	98
△	brown	T9	70	84	84	98
△	brown	T6	70	84	84	98
△	white	T9	140	168	168	196
△	white	T6	420	504	504	588
		Totals	840	1,008	1,008	1,176

20" block

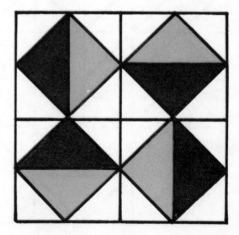

Templates	Color	Code	Number of pieces needed for quilt			
			Twin	Full	Queen	King
△	red	T11	40	40	50	60
△	red	T8	40	40	50	60
△	brown	T11	40	40	50	60
△	brown	T8	40	40	50	60
△	white	T11	80	80	100	120
△	white	T8	240	240	300	360
		Totals	480	480	600	720

4-patch

Total pieces in block: 24

Prairie Queen

*Like **Shoo-Fly** (page 66) and **Hour Glass** (page 60), this design is a popular variation of the basic **Nine-Patch**. Not much is known about its history, but this is a block which is beautiful when used alone—such as when one block is used for a pillow—as well as when it is used with several other blocks.*

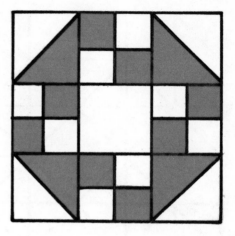

12" block

Templates	Color	Code	Number of pieces needed for quilt			
			Twin	Full	Queen	King
△	red	T6	216	288	288	360
□	red	S1	432	576	576	720
△	white	T6	216	288	288	360
□	white	S4	54	72	72	90
□	white	S1	432	576	576	720
		Totals	1,350	1,800	1,800	2,250

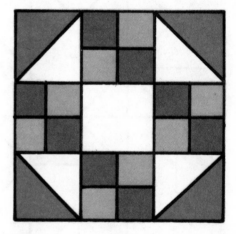

15" block

Templates	Color	Code	Number of pieces needed for quilt			
			Twin	Full	Queen	King
△	red	T8	140	168	168	224
□	red	S2	280	336	336	448
△	white	T8	140	168	168	224
□	white	S5	35	42	42	56
□	white	S2	280	336	336	448
		Totals	875	1,050	1,050	1,400

18" block

Templates	Color	Code	Number of pieces needed for quilt			
			Twin	Full	Queen	King
△	red	T10	96	120	120	144
□	red	S3	192	240	240	288
△	white	T10	96	120	120	144
□	white	S6	24	30	30	36
□	white	S3	192	240	240	288
		Totals	600	750	750	900

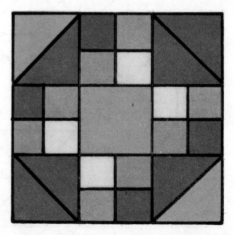

3-patch

Total pieces in block: 25

Steps-to-the-Altar

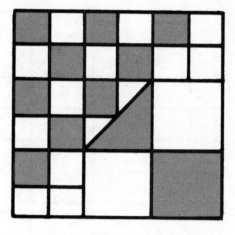

To prepare young women for marriage, mothers taught them how to clothe and care for their families. And what better way to keep a family warm than to make quilts! Custom dictated that, by the time a young woman actually climbed the steps to the altar, she had one dozen quilts in her hope chest.

Also illustrated in **Latticework** chapter, page 161.

12" block

Templates	Color	Code	Number of pieces needed for quilt			
			Twin	Full	Queen	King
□	green	S1	486	648	648	810
△	green	T6	54	72	72	90
□	green	S4	54	72	72	90
□	white	S1	648	864	864	1,080
△	white	T1	108	144	144	180
□	white	S4	108	144	144	180
		Totals	**1,458**	**1,944**	**1,944**	**2,430**

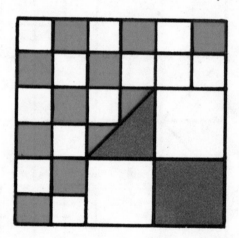

15" block

Templates	Color	Code	Number of pieces needed for quilt			
			Twin	Full	Queen	King
□	green	S2	315	378	378	504
△	green	T8	35	42	42	56
□	green	S5	35	42	42	56
□	white	S2	420	504	504	672
△	white	T2	70	84	84	112
□	white	S5	70	84	84	112
		Totals	**945**	**1,134**	**1,134**	**1,512**

18" block

Templates	Color	Code	Number of pieces needed for quilt			
			Twin	Full	Queen	King
□	green	S3	216	270	270	324
△	green	T10	24	30	30	36
□	green	S6	24	30	30	36
□	white	S3	288	360	360	432
△	white	T4	48	60	60	72
□	white	S6	48	60	60	72
		Totals	**648**	**810**	**810**	**972**

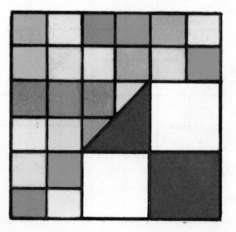

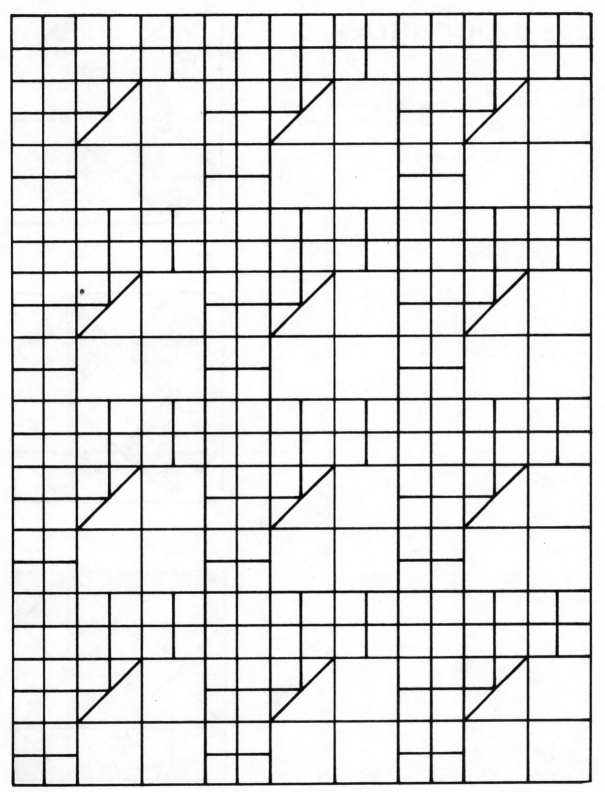

3-patch

Total pieces in block: 27

Old Tippecanoe

William Henry Harrison made his reputation fighting Indians in the early 1800's. His most famous battle was at Tippecanoe. In 1840, he was propelled into the Presidency with the slogan "Tippecanoe and Tyler, too." Although women were not allowed to vote in those days, one way they aired their views was through patchwork patterns such as this one.

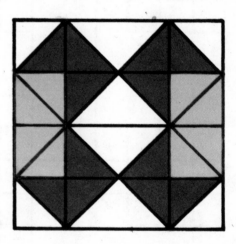

12″ block

Templates	Color	Code	Number of pieces needed for quilt			
			Twin	Full	Queen	King
△	red	T7	108	144	144	180
△	red	T4	432	576	576	720
△	black	T4	432	576	576	720
△	white	T7	108	144	144	180
△	white	T4	432	576	576	720
		Totals	1,512	2,016	2,016	2,520

16″ block

Templates	Color	Code	Number of pieces needed for quilt			
			Twin	Full	Queen	King
△	red	T9	70	84	84	98
△	red	T6	280	336	336	392
△	black	T6	280	336	336	392
△	white	T9	70	84	84	98
△	white	T6	280	336	336	392
		Totals	980	1,176	1,176	1,372

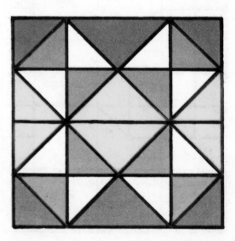

20″ block

Templates	Color	Code	Number of pieces needed for quilt			
			Twin	Full	Queen	King
△	red	T11	40	40	50	60
△	red	T8	160	160	200	240
△	black	T8	160	160	200	240
△	white	T11	40	40	50	60
△	white	T8	160	160	200	240
		Totals	560	560	700	840

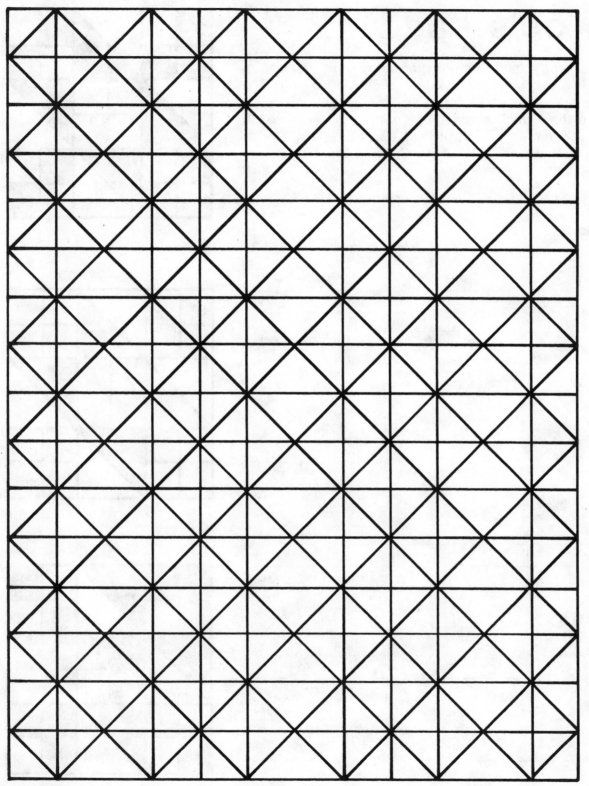

4-patch

Total pieces in block: 28

Jacob's Ladder

*Religion motivated the naming of many quilt designs
and this one, traditionally pieced in navy and white,
was popular in America's pre-Revolutionary days.
When a third color is added, the pattern becomes*
**Stepping-Stones, The-Tail-of-Benjamin's-Kite, The Underground
Railroad, Trail-of-the-Covered-Wagon,** *or*
Wagon-Trails.

Also illustrated in **Rotated Block** *chapter, page 172.*

12″ block

Templates	Color	Code	Number of pieces needed for quilt			
			Twin	Full	Queen	King
□	blue	S1	540	720	720	900
△	blue	T6	216	288	288	360
□	white	S1	540	720	720	900
△	white	T6	216	288	288	360
		Totals	1,512	2,016	2,016	2,520

15″ block

Templates	Color	Code	Number of pieces needed for quilt			
			Twin	Full	Queen	King
□	blue	S2	350	420	420	560
△	blue	T8	140	168	168	224
□	white	S2	350	420	420	560
△	white	T8	140	168	168	224
		Totals	980	1,176	1,176	1,568

18″ block

Templates	Color	Code	Number of pieces needed for quilt			
			Twin	Full	Queen	King
□	blue	S3	240	300	300	360
△	blue	T10	96	120	120	144
□	white	S3	240	300	300	360
△	white	T10	96	120	120	144
		Totals	672	840	840	1,008

3-patch

Total pieces in block: 28

Barbara Frietchie Star

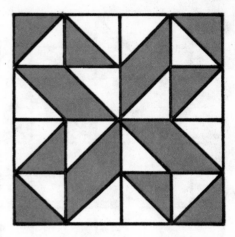

Barbara Frietchie courageously defied invading Confederate troops and was immortalized in the John Greenleaf Whittier poem that bears her name: "Shoot, if you must, this old gray head, But spare our country's flag, she said." Her contemporaries named this block for her.

Also illustrated in **Latticework** *chapter, page 159.*

12″ block

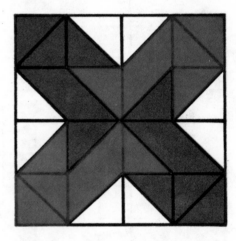

Templates	Color	Code	Number of pieces needed for quilt			
			Twin	Full	Queen	King
▱	blue	P1	216	288	288	360
△	blue	T4	432	576	576	720
△	white	T4	864	1,152	1,152	1,440
		Totals	**1,512**	**2,016**	**2,016**	**2,520**

16″ block

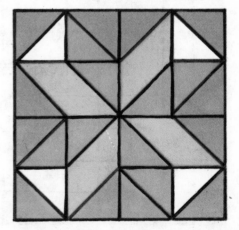

Templates	Color	Code	Number of pieces needed for quilt			
			Twin	Full	Queen	King
▱	blue	P2	140	168	168	196
△	blue	T6	280	336	336	392
△	white	T6	560	672	672	784
		Totals	**980**	**1,176**	**1,176**	**1,372**

20″ block

Templates	Color	Code	Number of pieces needed for quilt			
			Twin	Full	Queen	King
▱	blue	P3*	80	80	100	120
△	blue	T8	160	160	200	240
△	white	T8	320	320	400	480
		Totals	**560**	**560**	**700**	**840**

*Template outline not provided.

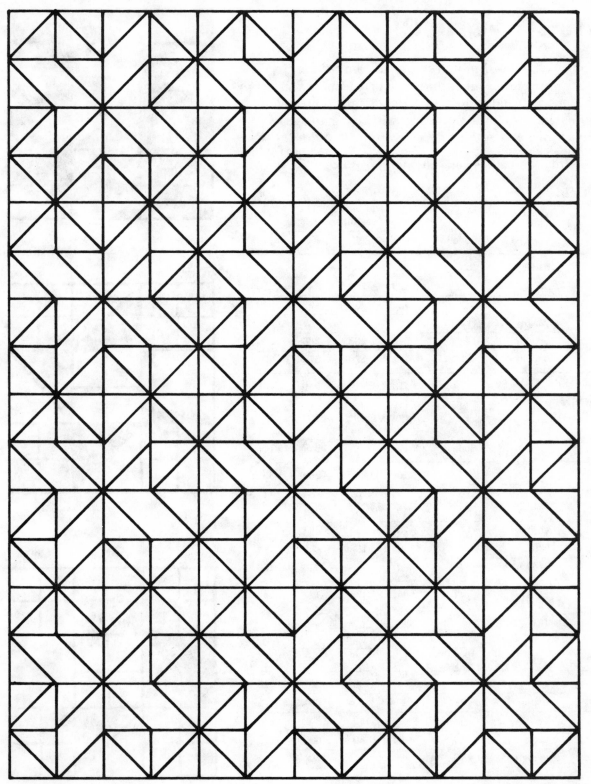

4-patch

Total pieces in block: 28

Water-Wheel

Even today, some old mills remain to remind us of their past importance in supplying early Americans with the power needed to grind wheat into flour. This simple design is surprisingly suggestive of a mill's wheel with drops of water flowing from its blades.

Also illustrated in **Latticework** *chapter, page 157.*

12" Block

| Templates | Color | Code | Number of pieces needed for quilt | | | |
			Twin	Full	Queen	King
□	orange	S1	324	432	432	540
△	orange	T6	108	144	144	180
□	yellow	S1	324	432	432	540
△	yellow	T6	108	144	144	180
△	brown	T6	216	288	288	360
□	brown	S1	432	576	576	720
		Totals	**1,512**	**2,016**	**2,016**	**2,520**

15" block

| Templates | Color | Code | Number of pieces needed for quilt | | | |
			Twin	Full	Queen	King
□	orange	S2	210	252	252	336
△	orange	T8	70	84	84	112
□	yellow	S2	210	252	252	336
△	yellow	T8	70	84	84	112
△	brown	T8	140	168	168	224
□	brown	S2	280	336	336	448
		Totals	**980**	**1,176**	**1,176**	**1,568**

18" block

| Templates | Color | Code | Number of pieces needed for quilt | | | |
			Twin	Full	Queen	King
□	orange	S3	144	180	180	216
△	orange	T10	48	60	60	72
□	yellow	S3	144	180	180	216
△	yellow	T10	48	60	60	72
△	brown	T10	96	120	120	144
□	brown	S3	192	240	240	288
		Totals	**672**	**840**	**840**	**1,008**

3-patch

Total pieces in block: 28

Eight-Pointed Star

Before city lights burned as brightly as they do today, partially obscuring the night sky, the stars were seen in all their glory. This inspiring sight led to quilt names like **Stars-and-Planets, Milky Way, Double-Starry,** and **Prairie Star.**

12″ block

Templates	Color	Code	Number of pieces needed for quilt			
			Twin	Full	Queen	King
□	brown	S4	54	72	72	90
△	brown	T1	432	576	576	720
△	brown	T3	216	288	288	360
□	white	S4	216	288	288	360
△	white	T1	432	576	576	720
△	white	T3	216	288	288	360
		Totals	**1,566**	**2,088**	**2,088**	**2,610**

15″ block

Templates	Color	Code	Number of pieces needed for quilt			
			Twin	Full	Queen	King
□	brown	S5	35	42	42	56
△	brown	T2	280	336	336	448
△	brown	T5	140	168	168	224
□	white	S5	140	168	168	224
△	white	T2	280	336	336	448
△	white	T5	140	168	168	224
		Totals	**1,015**	**1,218**	**1,218**	**1,624**

18″ block

Templates	Color	Code	Number of pieces needed for quilt			
			Twin	Full	Queen	King
□	brown	S6	24	30	30	36
△	brown	T4	192	240	240	288
△	brown	T7	96	120	120	144
□	white	S6	96	120	120	144
△	white	T4	192	240	240	288
△	white	T7	96	120	120	144
		Totals	**696**	**870**	**870**	**1,044**

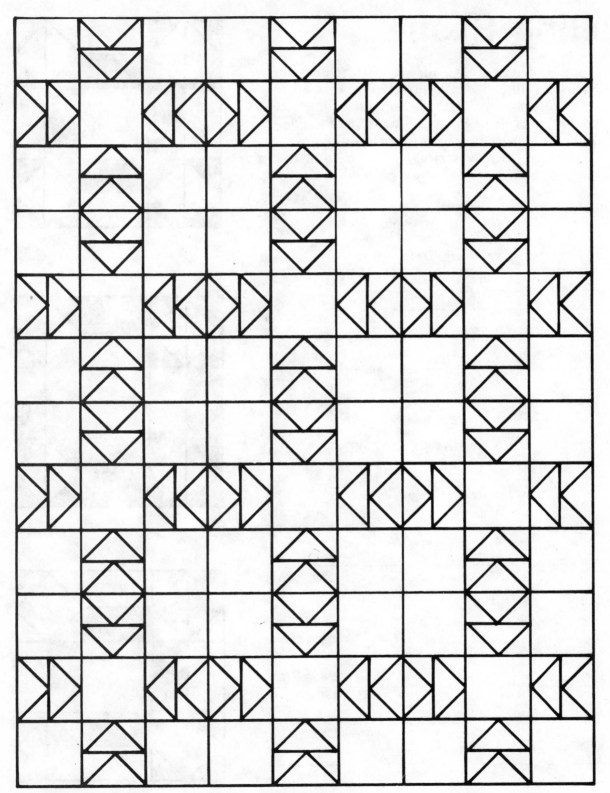

3-patch

Total pieces in block: 29

Rolling Stone

Maxims and proverbs were widely shared features of early American culture, due in no small part to such popular reading material as Poor Richard's Almanac. Many of these moralistic sayings—including the one which provided the name for this design—are still widely known. As anyone can tell you, "A rolling stone gathers no moss."

12" block

Templates	Color	Code	Number of pieces needed for quilt			
			Twin	Full	Queen	King
△	purple	T1	864	1,152	1,152	1,440
▭	purple	R1	216	288	288	360
△	white	T3	432	576	576	720
▭	white	R1	216	288	288	360
□	white	S4	54	72	72	90
		Totals	**1,782**	**2,376**	**2,376**	**2,970**

15" block

Templates	Color	Code	Number of pieces needed for quilt			
			Twin	Full	Queen	King
△	purple	T2	560	672	672	896
▭	purple	R2	140	168	168	224
△	white	T5	280	336	336	448
▭	white	R2	140	168	168	224
□	white	S5	35	42	42	56
		Totals	**1,155**	**1,386**	**1,386**	**1,848**

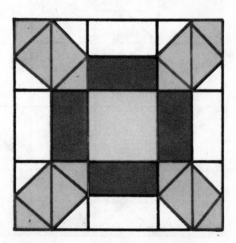

18" block

Templates	Color	Code	Number of pieces needed for quilt			
			Twin	Full	Queen	King
△	purple	T4	384	480	480	576
▭	purple	R3	96	120	120	144
△	white	T7	192	240	240	288
▭	white	R3	96	120	120	144
□	white	S6	24	30	30	36
		Totals	**792**	**990**	**990**	**1,188**

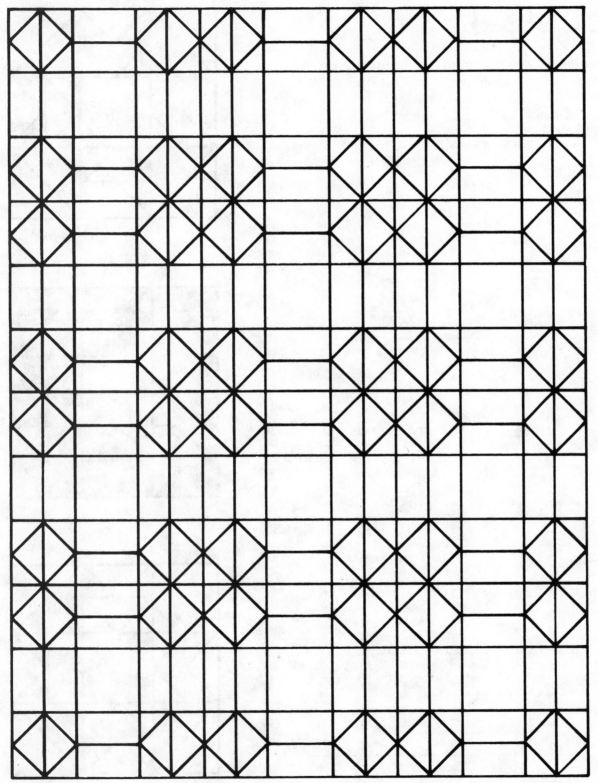

3-patch

Total pieces in block: 33

Double T

Created during the mid-ninteenth century in North Carolina, this design is also named **T-Blocks.** The letter T was also used to identify other designs such as **Mixed-T, Turnabout T,** and **Capital T.**

Also illustrated in **Latticework** chapter, page 158.

12″ block

Templates	Color	Code	Number of pieces needed for quilt			
			Twin	Full	Queen	King
△	pink	T6	216	288	288	360
△	pink	T1	864	1,152	1,152	1,440
△	white	T6	216	288	.288	360
□	white	S4	54	72	72	90
△	white	T3	432	576	576	720
		Totals	1,782	2,376	2,376	2,970

15″ block

Templates	Color	Code	Number of pieces needed for quilt			
			Twin	Full	Queen	King
△	pink	T8	140	168	168	224
△	pink	T2	560	672	672	896
△	white	T8	140	168	168	224
□	white	S5	35	42	42	56
△	white	T5	280	336	336	448
		Totals	1,155	1,386	1,386	1,848

18″ block

Templates	Color	Code	Number of pieces needed for quilt			
			Twin	Full	Queen	King
△	pink	T10	96	120	120	144
△	pink	T4	384	480	480	576
△	white	T10	96	120	120	144
□	white	S6	24	30	30	36
△	white	T7	192	240	240	288
		Totals	792	990	990	1,188

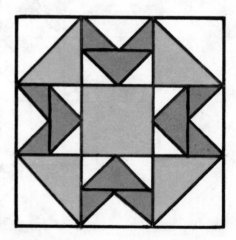

3-patch

Total pieces in block: 33

Cat's Cradle

Think back to when you were a child and played this string game, and then imagine pioneer children, without manufactured toys, picking up a bit of string and amusing themselves by the hour. Freed to do their daily chores, women showed their gratitude by naming a quilt after the game.

Also illustrated in **Rotated Block** *chapter, page 173.*

12″ block

| Templates | Color | Code | Number of pieces needed for quilt | | | |
			Twin	Full	Queen	King
□	green	S4	108	144	144	180
△	green	T6	324	432	432	540
△	yellow	T1	324	432	432	540
□	white	S4	54	72	72	90
△	white	T1	972	1,296	1,296	1,620
		Totals	**1,782**	**2,376**	**2,376**	**2,970**

15″ block

| Templates | Color | Code | Number of pieces needed for quilt | | | |
			Twin	Full	Queen	King
□	green	S5	70	84	84	112
△	green	T8	210	252	252	336
△	yellow	T2	210	252	252	336
□	white	S5	35	42	42	56
△	white	T2	630	756	756	1,008
		Totals	**1,155**	**1,386**	**1,386**	**1,848**

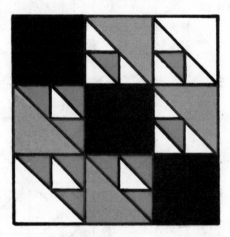

18″ block

| Templates | Color | Code | Number of pieces needed for quilt | | | |
			Twin	Full	Queen	King
□	green	S6	48	60	60	72
△	green	T10	144	180	180	216
△	yellow	T4	144	180	180	216
□	white	S6	24	30	30	36
△	white	T4	432	540	540	648
		Totals	**792**	**990**	**990**	**1,188**

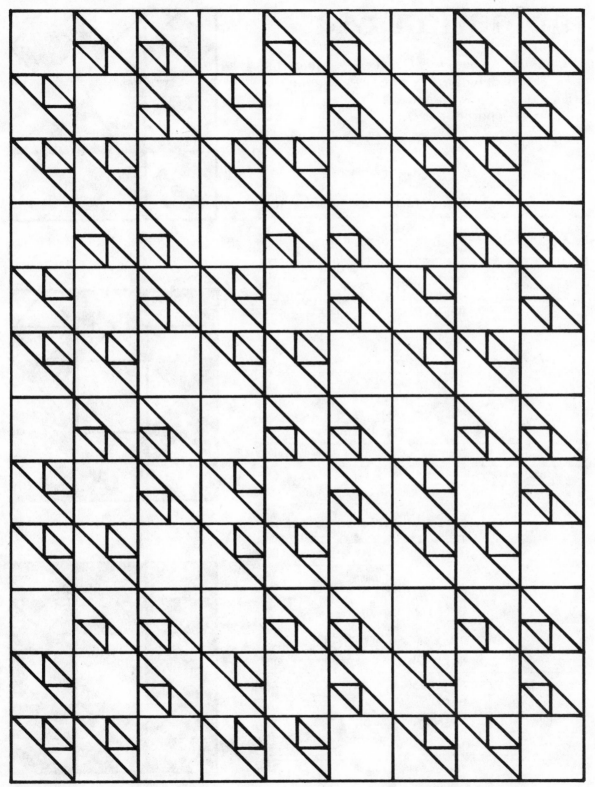

3-patch

Total pieces in block: 33

Combination Star

Another name for this design is **Ornate Star**—and well named it is. This is one of the most time-consuming block designs to use for a patchwork quilt because each block has 41 separate pieces!

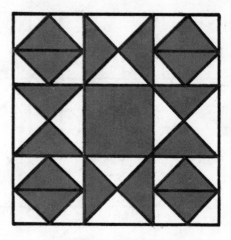

12" block

Templates	Color	Code	Number of pieces needed for quilt			
			Twin	Full	Queen	King
△	purple	T3	864	1,152	1,152	1,440
□	purple	S4	54	72	72	90
△	white	T3	432	576	576	720
△	white	T1	864	1,152	1,152	1,440
		Totals	2,214	2,952	2,952	3,690

15" block

Templates	Color	Code	Number of pieces needed for quilt			
			Twin	Full	Queen	King
△	purple	T5	560	672	672	896
□	purple	S5	35	42	42	56
△	white	T5	280	336	336	448
△	white	T2	560	672	672	896
		Totals	1,435	1,722	1,722	2,296

18" block

Templates	Color	Code	Number of pieces needed for quilt			
			Twin	Full	Queen	King
△	purple	T7	384	480	480	576
□	purple	S6	24	30	30	36
△	white	T7	192	240	240	288
△	white	T4	384	480	480	576
		Totals	984	1,230	1,230	1,476

3-patch

Total pieces in block: 41

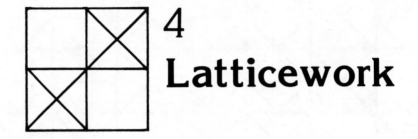

4
Latticework

In the *Color and Design* chapter we examined the ways blocks work together to form designs that are not apparent when looking at a single block, and we explored methods of making this design phenomenon work for you.

You may decide, however, that you do not want the blocks to form an integrated design spreading across the quilt top, but would rather have each block remain visually distinct. Using lattice is perhaps the easiest and most effective way to accomplish this.

Lattice—strips of fabric set between the individual blocks—forms a framework around each block. This separation of the blocks is effective when a relatively simple block design is done in several different fabrics or when the quilt top is composed of complex blocks that are seen to best advantage when set apart.

The color of the lattice strips must be carefully chosen, for it will have a strong impact on the total look of the quilt top. If one of the predominant colors in the block is also used for the lattice, the lattice and that portion of the block will "read together" and dominate the design formed on the quilt top. Compare the effect of the brown lattice used with the **Road-to-Oklahoma** blocks (*Illustration 56*) with that of the pink lattice used with the same blocks (*Illustration 57*).

Illustration 56
Road-to-Oklahoma

Illustration 57
Road-to-Oklahoma

When the lattice color is not used in the design, for example the brown used in the **Road-to-Oklahoma** blocks, it does not read with any color in the design and the blocks appear distinct from the lattice. If the color used for the lattice is the same as the color used for the background in the block, the background and lattice read together. In the **Water-Wheel** blocks below, notice that the central motif appears to be suspended against the brown background (*Illustration 58*).

Illustration 58
Water Wheel

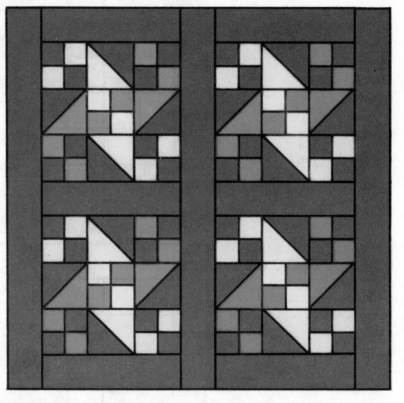

You may want to set each block apart and yet have the design flow across the quilt top. One way to do this is to allow some facet of the design to continue across the intersection of the lattice. In this set of **Road-to-Oklahoma** blocks, corner squares interrupt the lattice to connect the blocks visually (*Illustration 59*).

This continuation of the design need not occur at the intersection of the lattice. Its placement can be determined by the design of the block itself, as with these **Water-Wheel** blocks where the central motif from the block interrupts the lattice at the middle of the blocks, rather than at the corners (*Illustration 60*).

Illustration 59
Road-to-Oklahoma

Illustration 60
Water Wheel

Planning a latticework quilt

If you have chosen to make a latticework quilt, do not use the Designer's Worksheet until *after* you have used the chart below to determine the number of blocks in the standard size lattice-work quilt. When you use lattice between the blocks, the total number of blocks required for your quilt decreases because of the space taken up by the lattice.

We have listed below the best block size to use for a lat-ticework quilt in each of the standard quilt sizes. Since not all block sizes fit nicely into a latticework quilt, we suggest that you use the appropriate chart (determined by whether your block is a three- or four-patch design) and select a block in the size listed.

Latticework chart for three-patch blocks

	Block size	Lattice width	Number of blocks needed for quilt	Border measurement	Finished quilt size
Twin	15″	3″	4 × 6 = 24	7″ x 7″	83″ x 112″
Full	15″	3″	5 × 6 = 30	8½″ x 7″	98″ x 112″
Queen	15″	4″	5 × 6 = 30	6½″ x 7″	104″ x 117″
King	12″	5″	6 × 7 = 42	9½″ x 7″	116″ x 121″

Latticework chart for four-patch blocks

	Block size	Lattice width	Number of blocks needed for quilt	Border measurement	Finished quilt size
Twin	16″	5″	3 × 5 = 15	12½″ x 12″	83″ x 112″
Full	16″	5″	4 × 5 = 20	9½″ x 12″	98″ x 112″
Queen	16″	3″	5 × 6 = 30	6″ x 6″	104″ x 117″
King	12″	5″	6 × 7 = 42	9½″ x 7″	116″ x 121″

Be sure, when you make the grid for your quilt, to include the placement of the lattice. Illustration 61 is the grid for a queen-size latticework quilt made with a four-patch block. The easiest way to make your grid is to trace or copy the outlines of the individual blocks from the grid provided on the block-design page. Add the number of blocks necessary to match the number you will be using, which will undoubtedly be more than the twelve shown on that grid. Allow extra space around the edges for a border.

Illustration 61

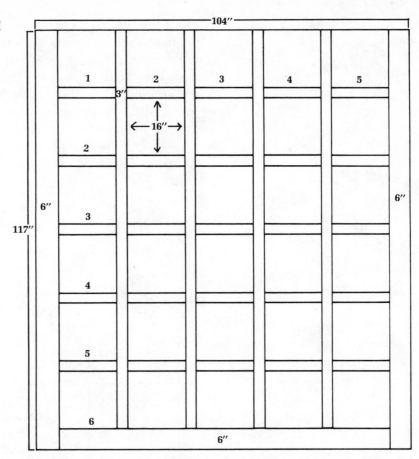

Construction The construction of a latticework quilt is similar to that of a quilt in which the blocks are set directly next to each other. However, you will have to cut out the lattice strips as well as the patches for each block.

Lattice strips running the length of the quilt should be in one continuous piece, equal in length to the length of the quilt top plus a ¾" seam allowance (⅜" on *each* end.) Lattice strips running the width of the quilt should be equal in length to the width of *one block* plus ¾" (⅜" on each end) for the seam allowance. You must also allow ¾" for the seams on the long edges of the lattice strips.

Once you have determined the length of each lattice strip (including the seam allowance) measure this amount on the wrong side of your fabric. If the fabric tears easily and straight, simply tear the fabric into equal strips.

For the quilt shown in the grid above, we would need four strips measuring 3¾" (remember, ¾" is added for the seam allowances) x 117¾" and twenty strips measuring 3¾" x 16¾" for the interior latticework, and one strip measuring 6¾" x

$104\frac{3}{4}''$ plus two strips measuring $6\frac{3}{4}'' \times 117\frac{3}{4}''$ for the borders.

Begin your latticework quilt by making the individual blocks and cutting out the strips. Then lay out the quilt top, using the blocks and strips as indicated on your grid. Piece the blocks and short strips together forming a row that extends the length of the quilt. Once these rows are completed, sew the long seams which run the length of the quilt to join the rows of blocks and the lattice strips. Attach the bottom border to the body of the quilt. Finish by adding the side borders (*Illustration 62*).

Step 1

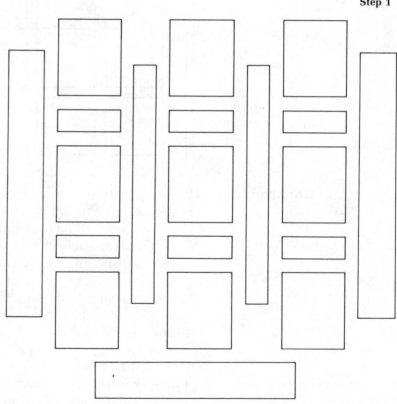

Illustration 62

In the grids which follow, lattice is used with some of the blocks which were introduced in Chapter 3, *50 Traditional Patchwork Designs*. The blocks used ranged from the relatively simple **Saw-Tooth**— a pattern often done in lattice with the background of each block in one color, but the star of each block in a different color—to **Steps-to-the-Altar,** a complex pattern which may be better appreciated when the blocks are separated by lattice. Of course, lattice can be used with any block of your choosing. The grids provided are merely examples to let you experiment and develop a feel for the different effects possible.

Step 2

Step 3

Step 4

Step 5

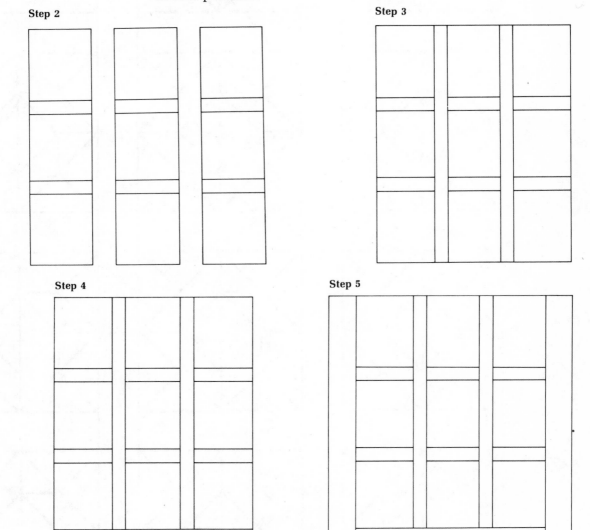

Windblown Square

Sawtooth

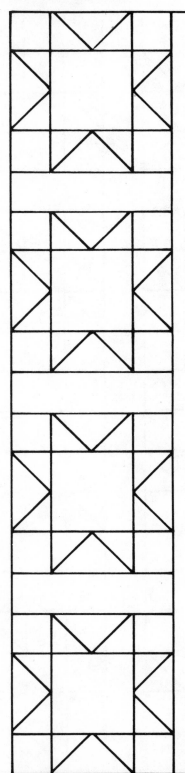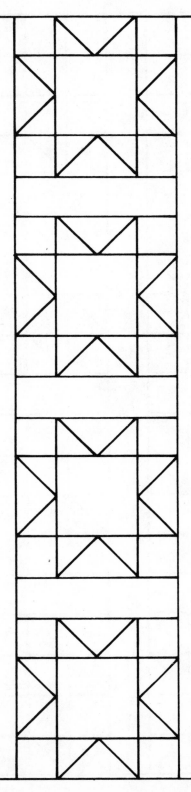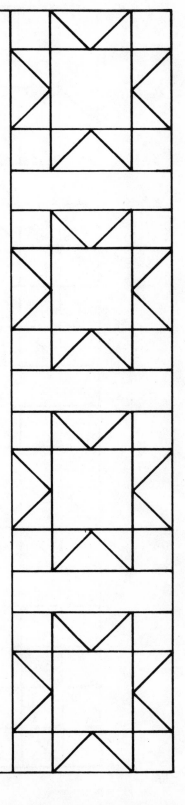

Road-to-Oklahoma

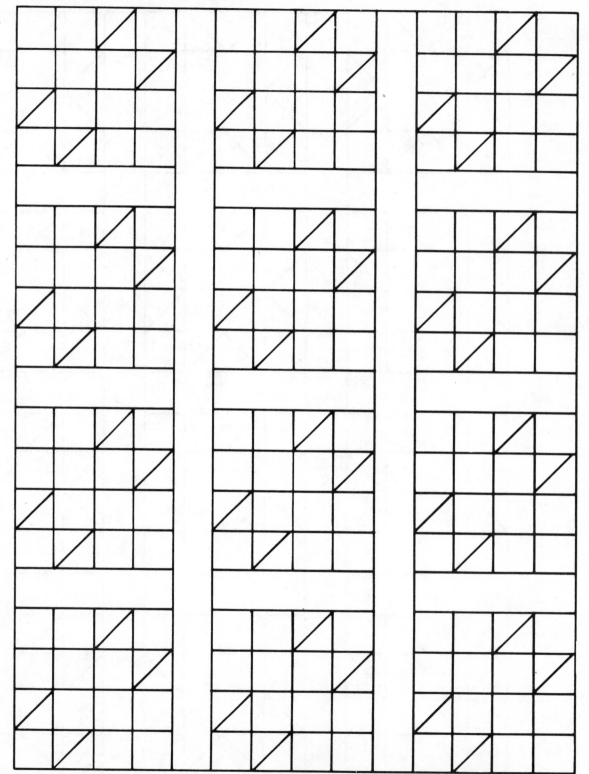

Water Wheel

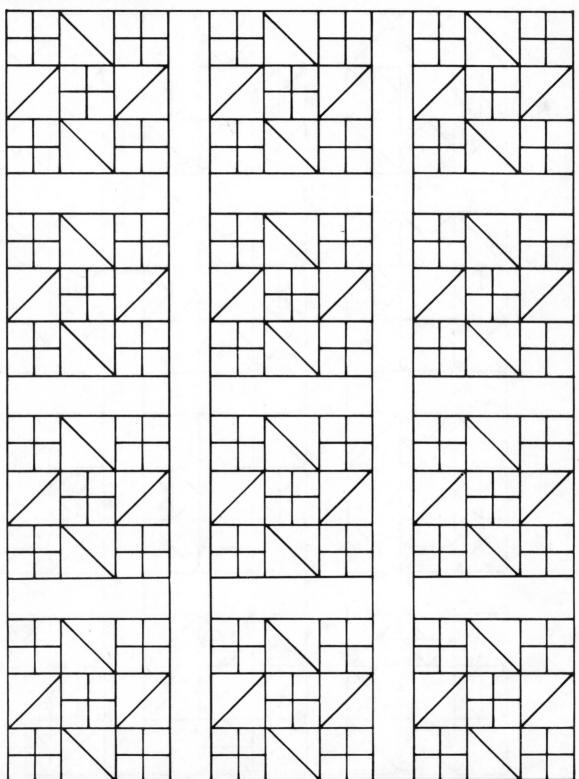

Double T

Barbara Frietchie Star

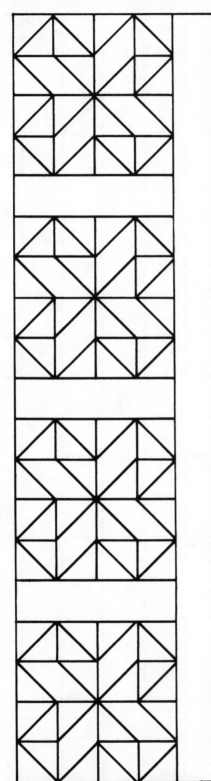
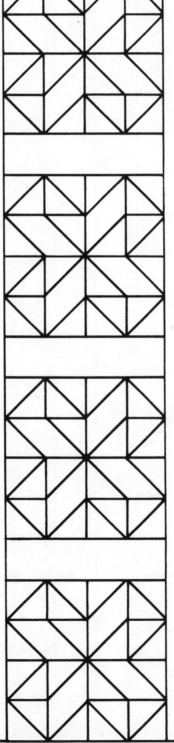
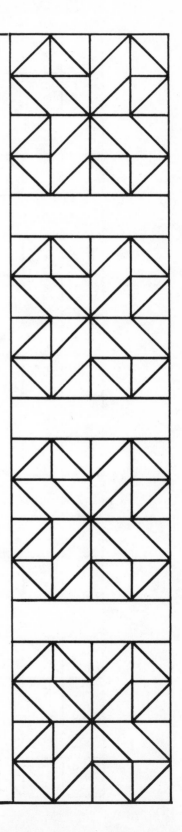

Pin-Wheel

Steps-to-the-Altar

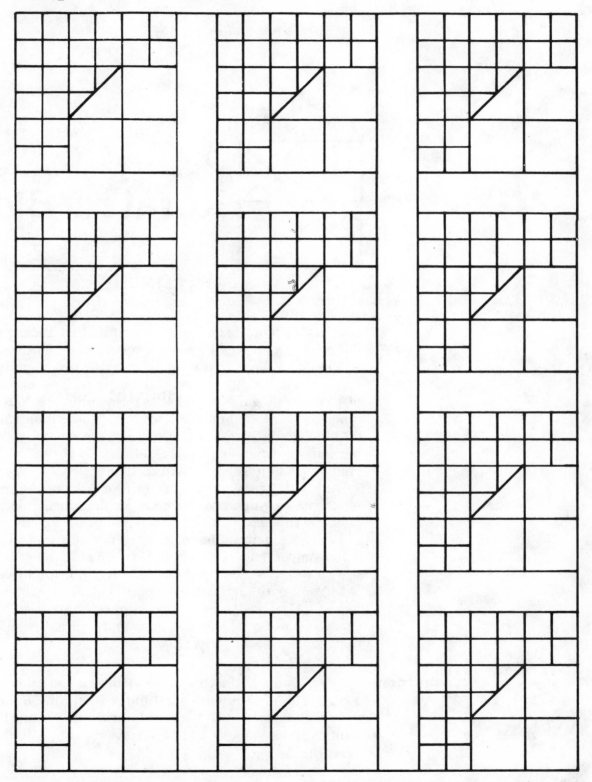

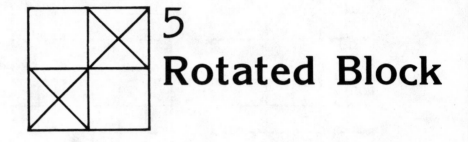

5 Rotated Block

Blocks which are not symmetrical form dramatically different designs when every other block rotates one-quarter turn. The blocks form larger patterns extended across four blocks or more. Compare the pattern formed by four blocks of **Flock-of-Geese** set regularly with that formed by four blocks every other block rotated one quarter-turn (*Illustration 63*).

Odd Fellows' Cross provides another example of the possible designs when blocks are rotated. Two examples of the many possibilities are shown in Illustration 64.

During the design stage, try to lose sight of the individual blocks and be open to the new, larger designs possible. Let your eye run across the grid, then pull back from the page and visualize as many different designs as you can.

Remember that the design you work out on this grid, consists of twelve blocks, and represents only a portion of your quilt top. Your quilt top will be composed of twenty to ninety blocks. If the design only repeats once on the grid, don't despair. It will be repeated several times on any standard-size quilt top.

Construction The construction of a rotated block quilt is the same as that of a regular quilt. The individual block is still the basic unit of construction. However, the use of a grid representing the entire quilt top (see page 30) becomes even more important as a blueprint.

Illustration 63
Flock-of-Geese

Blocks set regularly.

Set with blocks rotated.

Illustration 64
Odd Fellow's Cross

164

Odd Fellow's Cross

Old Maid's Puzzle

Flock-of-Geese

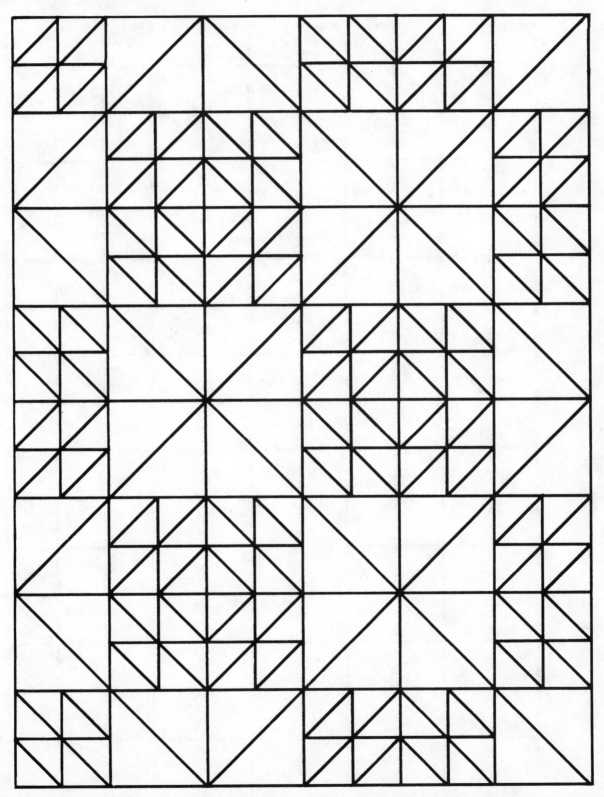

Road-to-Oklahoma

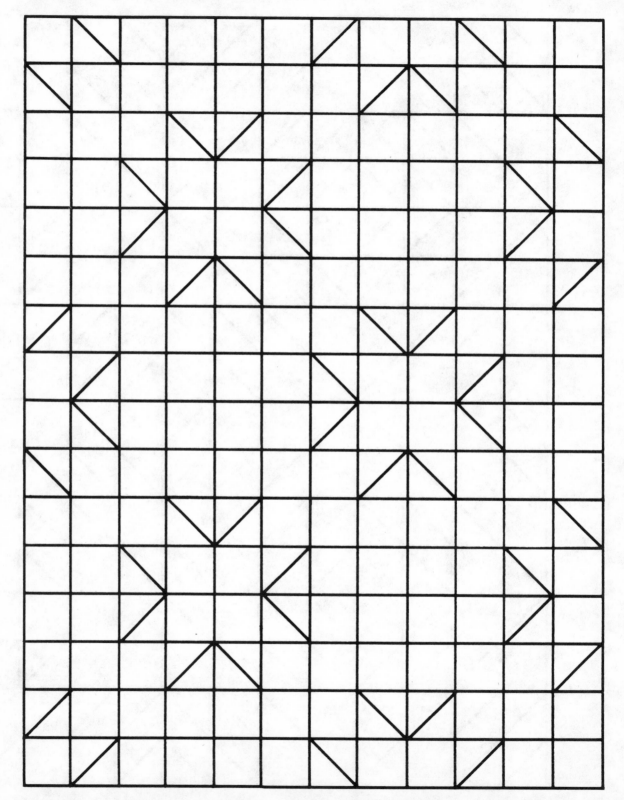

Ribbons

Hovering Hawks

Anvil

Jacob's Ladder

Cat's Cradle

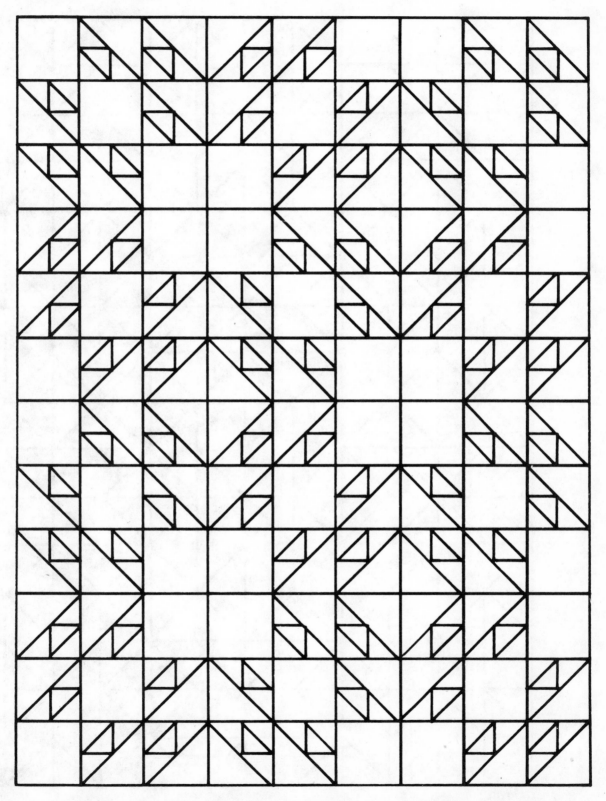

Brown Goose

6
Overall Designs

The designs in this chapter differ from the others in this book because they are not based on the use of one basic block design which is repeated to create the design on the quilt top. Rather, each design is based on the repetition of one—or at most two—templates and is conceived as a single entity covering the entire quilt top. The difference between these two approaches can be illustrated using the **Nine-Patch** block and the square template.

Because its few straight seams were easy to sew, the **Nine-Patch**—nine equal squares sewn together to form a block—was the block that many young girls used for their first quilt. A basic **Nine-Patch** design using a repeated block is shown in Illustration 65.

The following illustrations are popular designs created from squares which are not based on a block design such as the **Nine-Patch.** Rather, each design is conceived on a much larger scale to cover the quilt top. The repeated portion, if any, is much larger than that which results from the use of blocks. The pattern composed of concentric diamonds of squares (*Illustration 66*) is known by several names, the most common being

Illustration 65
Nine Patch

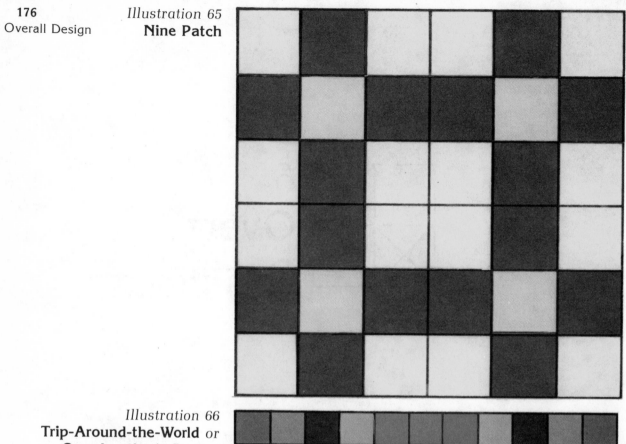

Illustration 66
Trip-Around-the-World *or*
Grandmother's Dream

Trip-Around-the-World and **Grandmother's Dream**. The **Double Irish Chain** (*Illustration 67*) is one of the **Irish Chain** designs which have enjoyed wide popularity. These designs are commonly seen with single, double, or triple "chains." The chains are the diagonal rows of dark squares. The solid color spaces created between the intersections of the chains are often filled with fancy quilting or appliqué.

Three other popular design variations based on the use of the square are **Streak-of-Lightning, Checkerboard** (*Illustration 68*), and **Hanging Diamond** (*Illustration 69*).

Barn Raising is sometimes termed a variant of the basic **Nine-Patch**. Each square is divided into two triangles. The triangles are colored to form concentric diamonds which are shaded alternately light and dark. The fabric in each square may vary randomly, or be in a precise pattern (*Illustration 70*).

The **Brick Wall** (*Illustration 71*) was a popular design with early quiltmakers because the size of the "bricks" could be varied depending upon the size of the scraps which were available. The colors in the traditional **Brick Wall** quilt alternate between light and dark. Note that the vertical seam of each block intersects the centers of the block in the rows above

Illustration 67
Double Irish Chain

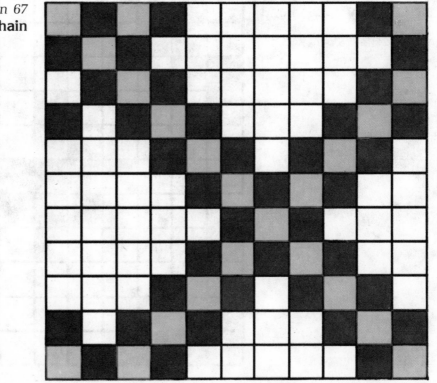

Illustration 68

UPPER LEFT:
Streak-of-Lightning

LOWER RIGHT:
Checkerboard

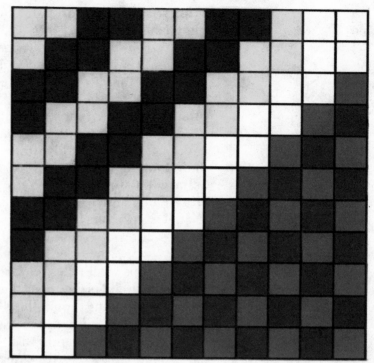

Illustration 69
Hanging Diamond

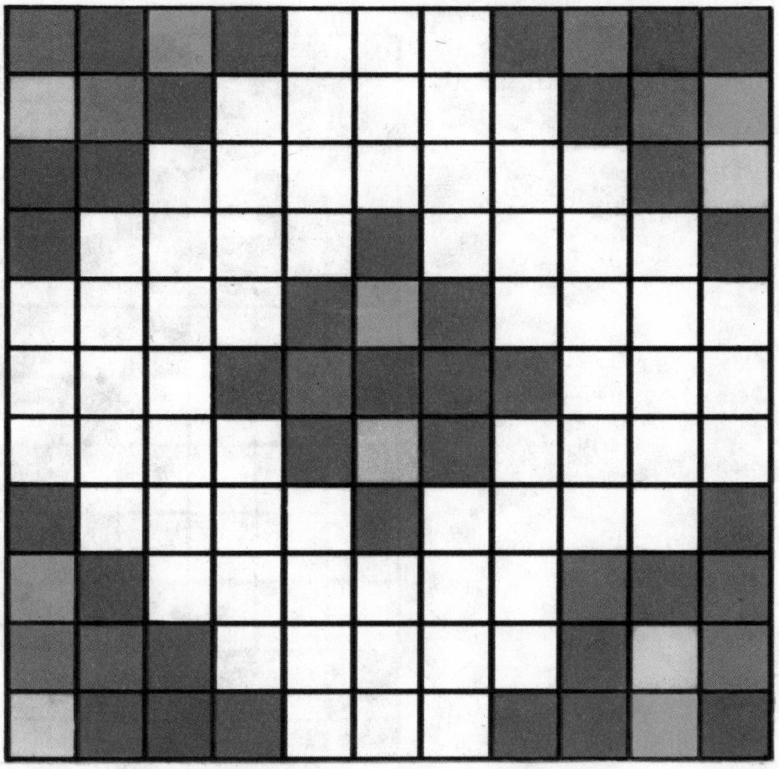

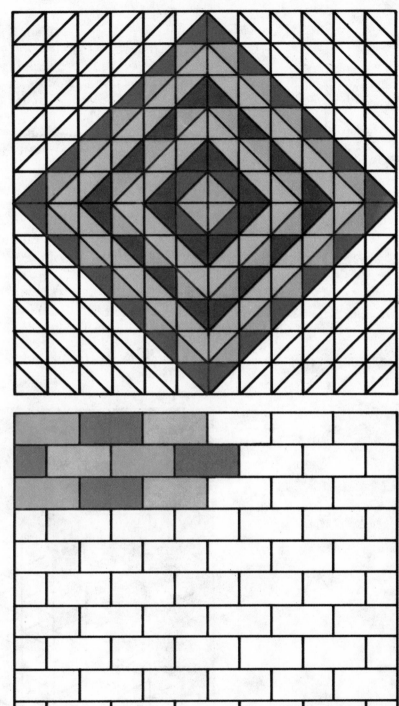

Illustration 70
Barn Raising

Illustration 71
Brick Wall

and below. A design very similar to **Brick Wall**—different only in that the seams match—was called simply **Hit-and-Miss** because of its random arrangement of color.

One Thousand Pyramids or **One Thousand Triangles** is a design composed solely of triangles. (See page 189.) It is another design which is effective with random color, yet which allows experimentation with the precise placement of color.

Another design composed solely of triangles is **Streak o' Lightning** (not to be confused with **Streak-of-Lightning,** shown in Illustration 68). This pattern—also with good reason called **Zig-Zag** or **Rail Fence**—is usually made from only two colors (*Illustration 72*).

Any four small squares on the grid labeled **Yankee Puzzle II** (page 191) equal the **Yankee Puzzle** block shown in the *50 Traditional Patchwork Designs* chapter. We have included a smaller-scale grid in this chapter to provide a better indication of the design possibilities when the design, composed solely of one-size triangles, is viewed as an overall design rather than one based on a block.

Another design fashioned only of triangles is **Wild Goose**

Illustration 72
Streak o' Lightning

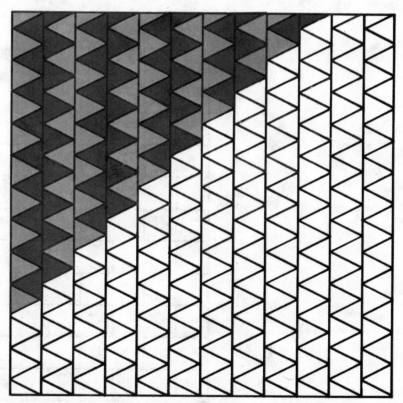

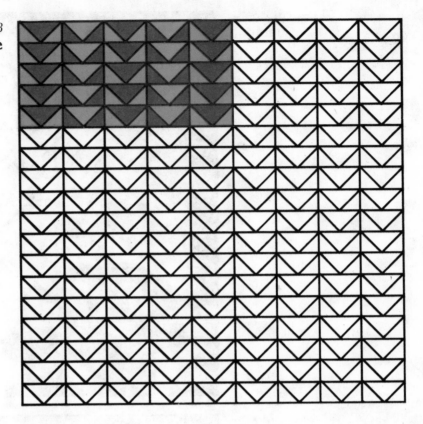

Illustration 73
Wild Goose Chase

Chase, traditionally done in two bright colors (Illustration 73).

Perhaps the most spectacular pattern based on the use of only one geometric shape is a **Sunburst** variation composed solely of parallelograms. While this design is most often shown with diamonds as the basic shape, we have chosen to use the parallelogram, which allows you to use one of the templates illustrated in this book. The illustrations which follow indicate the strikingly different effects which are possible through the use of color (*Illustrations 74 and 75*).

Planning an overall quilt

The most important step in planning an overall quilt is making a grid which shows the full number of patches you will be using, plus any borders.

Once you have made the grid, you can determine the number of patches of each color you will need simply by counting them as they appear. If you are using a very limited number of colors, you can count the number of each color template in the basic unit of the quilt and multiply this times the number of these units in the quilt. For example, in a traditional **Streak o'**

Illustration 74
Sunburst

Illustration 75
Sunburst

Lightning done in two colors, count the number of each color template in the strips which extend the length of the quilt and multiply this number by the number of strips in the entire quilt.

Construction

All of the overall designs in this chapter may be made from any size square, rectangle, triangle, or parallelogram illustrated in the *Template* chapter, with the exception of **Streak-of-Lightning** and **One Thousand Triangles.** Both of these designs are made with equilateral triangles (all three sides of the triangle are of equal length). If you choose these designs, you will have to make your own templates. All other designs are made with isosceles triangles (only two sides are equal) and are covered in the *Templates* chapter.

When constructing a quilt from blocks, you can adjust minor discrepancies in the shape or size of the blocks as you sew them together. However, when working with overall designs, in which construction is based on one large unit, you must be especially precise in your sewing, for it is more difficult to compensate as you go along.

The same general principles of construction used for quilt tops composed of blocks apply here as well:

■ Piece small units together to form larger units.
■ Plan the construction so that you need to sew only straight seams.
Several of these designs (**Streak o' Lightning, One Thousand Pyramids, Brick Wall,** and **Wild Goose Chase**) must be constructed by first piecing together strips the length or width of the quilt and then sewing the strips together. The **Sunburst** variation should be constructed by first dividing the quilt into sections (as in Illustration 76) and piecing these sections just as you would blocks. Some of the designs, such as **Barn Raising** or **Yankee Puzzle II,** can be pieced by either method.

A design composed of squares or rectangles is easier to sew than one composed of triangles or parallelograms because the fabric for a square or rectangle is cut only along the straight of the grain. The raw edges have little or no stretch. In a triangle or parallelogram, at least one side, if not two, is cut along the bias and will stretch if great care is not taken during the construction. (Because of this, you may want to baste the bias edges of triangles and parallelograms.)

We suggest that only experienced sewers attempt the **Sunburst** variation pattern, which is the most difficult of the patterns presented in this chapter. If you are considering using

Illustration 76
Sunburst Construction

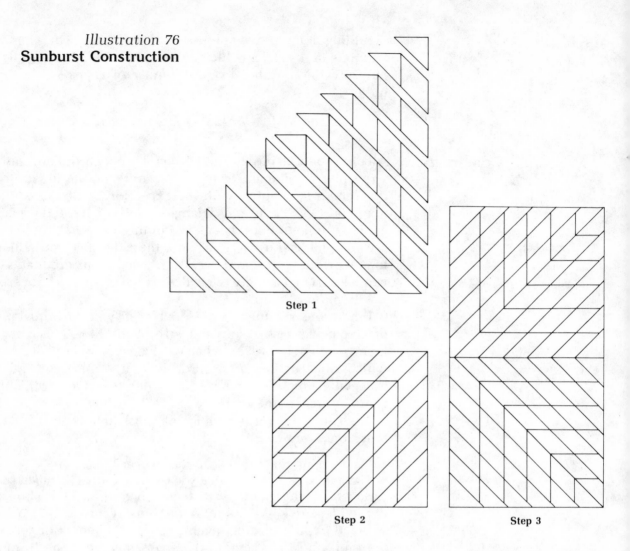

Step 1

Step 2

Step 3

this pattern, try a pillow or small item to test the technique and make sure that constructing a full-size quilt will be an enjoyable, as well as a successful, project for you.

If you decide to construct the **Sunburst** variation, plan your construction by following these instructions and Illustration 76:

1 Divide the design into quadrants.

2 Divide the quadrants in half from the center to the outside corner of the quilt.

3 Piece each of these areas just as you would a block, sewing the small pieces into strips, the strips into the half quadrants, the half quadrants into full quadrants, the quadrants together to make the whole.

Nine Patch

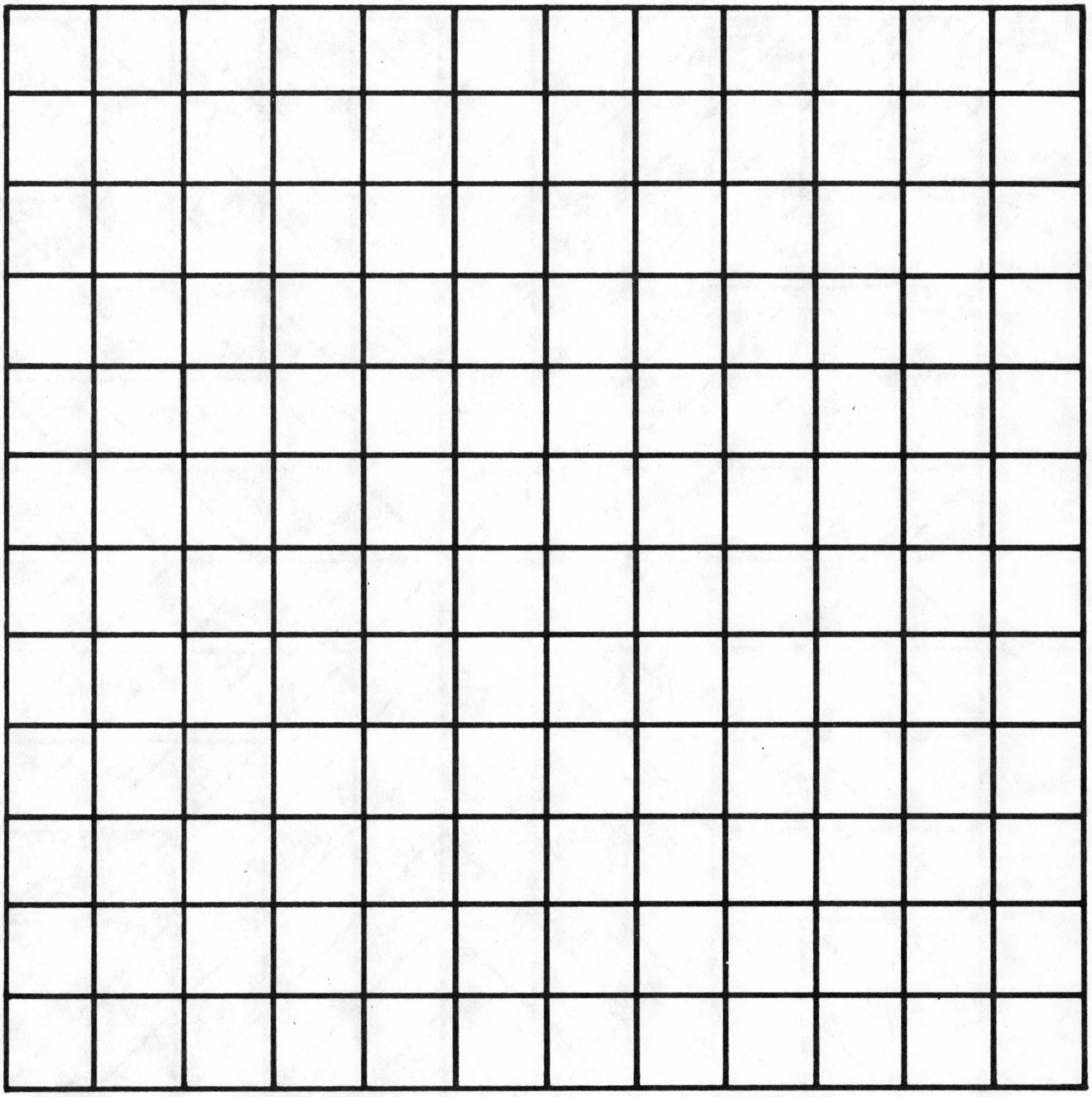

Sunburst

Barn Raising

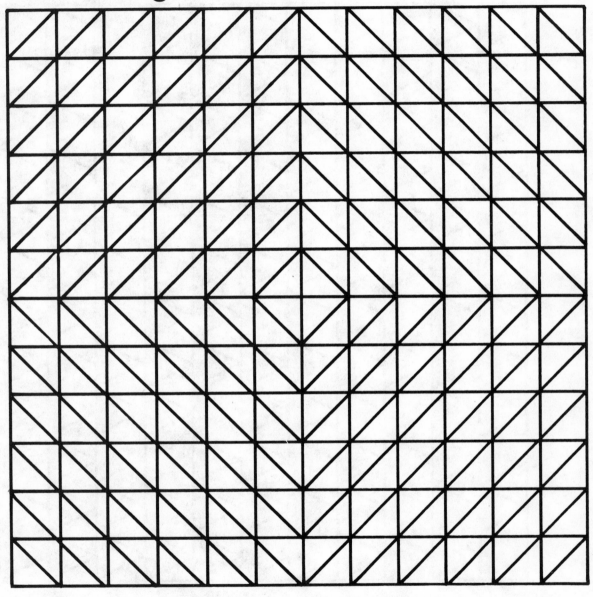

Streak o' Lightning

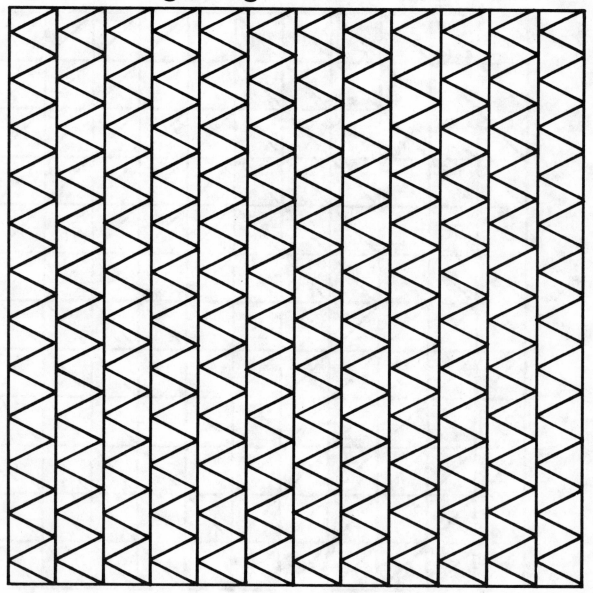

One Thousand Pyramids or
One Thousand Triangles

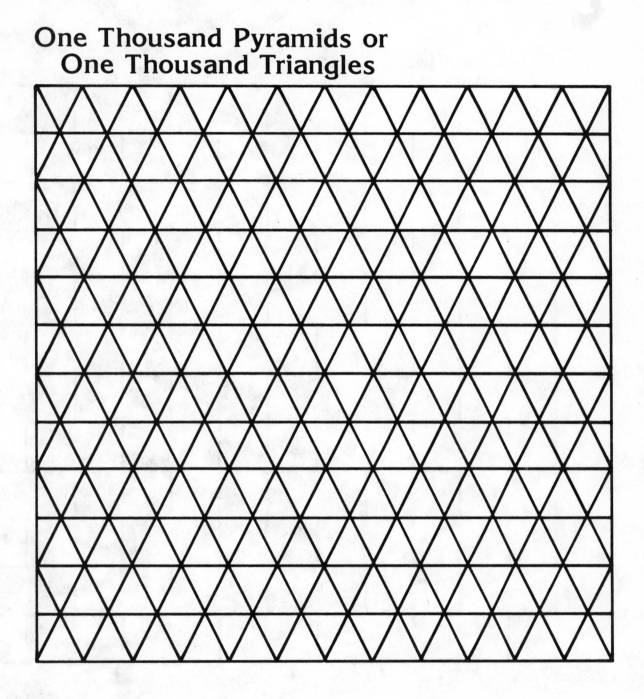

Brick Wall

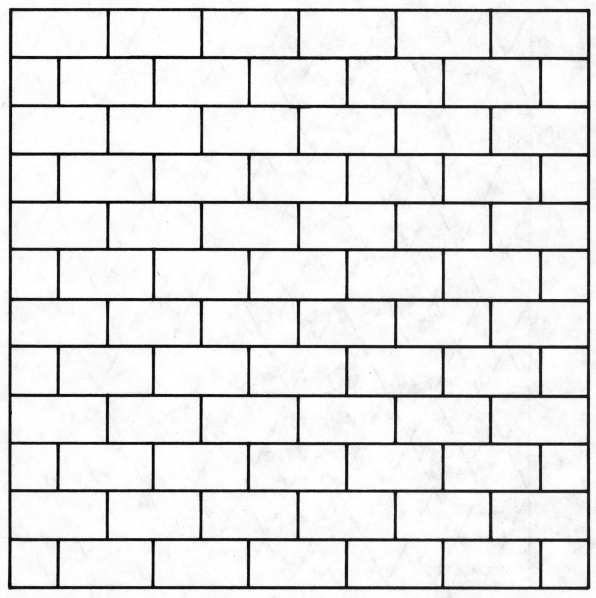

Yankee Puzzle II

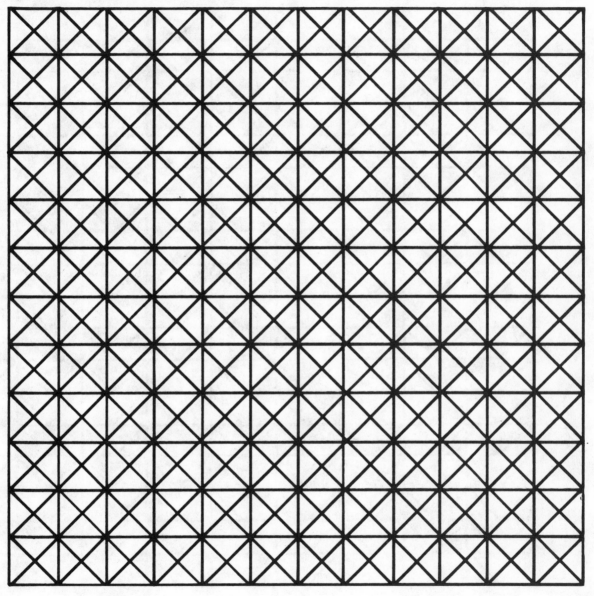

Wild Goose Chase

7 Designer's Worksheet

How to use the Designer's Worksheet

If you have chosen to use your own design or one of the illustrated color variations rather than one of the traditional blocks shown in this book, the Designer's Worksheet will help you determine what block size to use and how much fabric to acquire for each color in your design.

To illustrate how to use the Designer's Worksheet, we have chosen a variation of the traditional **Clay's Choice** block and will explain the use of the Worksheet step by step.

1 *Draw your design in the appropriate grid below.*

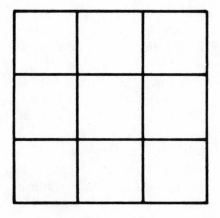 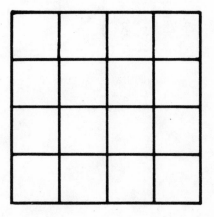

Each design in this book is either a three- or four-patch design and will fit only within the lines of the appropriate grid above. Each design is identified as either a three- or four-patch design on the page where it is first shown in the *50 Traditional Patchwork Designs* chapter. Since the grid above is composed only of the basic squares, you may have to draw diagonal lines to accomodate triangles or parallelograms, as we have done in our example.

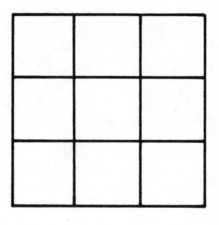 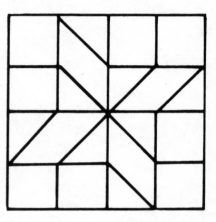

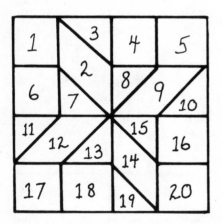

2 *Count the number of pieces in your design.* Count each shape (square, triangle, parallelogram) as one, as in illustration at left.

3 *Determine the finished size of the quilt* (Twin, full, queen, or king).

4 *Using the block chart on page 29, determine the block size you want to use for your quilt top.* The number of blocks required for a quilt top varies according to the size of the quilt and the size of the block. The Block Chart on page 29 indicates how many blocks are required for a standard-size quilt made from each of the block sizes for which templates are provided. To determine the total number of pieces in a quilt, simply multiply the number of blocks required by the number of pieces in each block.

For example, our block has 20 pieces and we intend to make a king-size quilt. Since this is a four-patch block, the sizes available are 12″, 16″, and 20″. Reference to the Block Chart shows that a king-size quilt requires the following number of blocks: 90 when made in 12″ blocks, 49 when made in 16″ blocks, and 30 when made in 20″ blocks. Thus, we will fill in the blanks provided as follows:

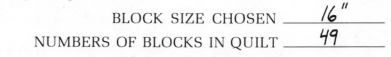

Number of pieces in the block		Number of blocks in the quilt		Total number of pieces
20	×	90 (12")	=	1800
20	×	49 (16")	=	980
20	×	30 (20")	=	600

As indicated on the Worksheet, the general guide for determining the degree of difficulty of a particular design is

> 250–500 pieces: beginner
> 500–750 pieces: intermediate
> Over 750 pieces: experienced

Since we are willing to construct a quilt of some difficulty, we have chosen to use the 16″ block which will form a quilt requiring 980 pieces.

BLOCK SIZE CHOSEN _____ _16″_

NUMBERS OF BLOCKS IN QUILT _____ _49_

5 *Using the diagram you drew in step 1 above, go to the* Templates *chapter beginning on page 199 and fill in the first six columns of the chart below. Note that there may be two different size triangles, or other templates of the same color. Each must be listed separately. Also, when using the template chart, remember that any given shape of template may be turned several different ways within the block and yet it is only one template and has only one code. For example, all of the triangles in* **Clay's Choice** *are in fact the same triangle.*

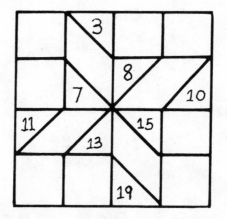

6 *Turn to the Yardage Charts beginning on page 215 and fill in columns seven and eight.*

7. *Total the yardage requirements for each color.*

1	2	3	4		5		6	7	8
Color	Template shape	Template Code	Number of this template in block	×	Number of blocks in quilt	=	Total number of this template	Yardage required 36″	45″
1. DARK BLUE	SQUARE	S3	4	×	49	=	196	2½	2
	PARALLELOGRAM	P1	4	×	49	=	196	4	3¼
				×		=			
				×		=		6½	5¼
2. LT. BLUE	SQUARE	S3	4	×	49	=	196	2½	2
	TRIANGLE	T4	4	×	49	=	196	2	1¾
				×		=			
				×		=		4½	3¾
3. WHITE	TRIANGLE	T4	4	×	49	=	196	2	1¾
				×		=			
				×		=			
				×		=		2	1¾
4.				×		=			
				×		=			
				×		=			
				×		=			

Designer's Worksheet

1 DRAW YOUR DESIGN IN THE APPROPRIATE GRID BELOW.

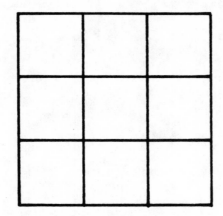 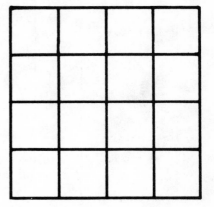

2 COUNT THE NUMBER OF PIECES IN YOUR DESIGN. _____

3 DETERMINE THE FINISHED SIZE OF THE QUILT (Twin, full, queen, or king). _____

4 USING THE BLOCK CHART ON PAGE 29, DETERMINE THE BLOCK SIZE YOU WANT TO USE FOR YOUR QUILT TOP.

Number of pieces in the block		Number of blocks in the quilt		Total number of pieces
_____	×	_____	=	_____
_____	×	_____	=	_____
_____	×	_____	=	_____

General Guide:

250–500 pieces: beginner
500–750 pieces: intermediate
Over 750 pieces: experienced

BLOCK SIZE CHOSEN _____

NUMBER OF BLOCKS IN QUILT _____

5 USING THE DIAGRAM YOU DREW IN STEP 1 ABOVE, GO TO THE TEMPLATE CHAPTER BEGINNING ON PAGE 199 AND FILL IN THE FIRST SIX COLUMNS OF THE CHART BELOW.

6 TURN TO THE YARDAGE CHARTS BEGINNING ON PAGE 215 AND FILL IN COLUMNS SEVEN AND EIGHT.

7 TOTAL THE YARDAGE REQUIREMENTS FOR EACH COLOR.

1	2	3	4	5	6	7	8
						Yardage required	
Color	Template shape	Template Code	Number of this template in block	Number of blocks in quilt	Total number of this template	36″	45″
1.			×	=			
			×	=			
			×	=			
			×	=			
2.			×	=			
			×	=			
			×	=			
			×	=			
3.			×	=			
			×	=			
			×	=			
			×	=			
4.			×	=			
			×	=			
			×	=			
			×	=			

8
Templates

The most important thing to remember when piecing together a patchwork quilt by machine is to make accurate template patterns. If your template is inaccurate by as little as $\frac{1}{8}''$, it will be difficult, if not impossible, to sew the blocks together so that all the corners match. If your patches are too small or too large, the finished edges of your carefully planned quilt will not be even.

As we mentioned in the *Putting It All Together* chapter, you will be using the marking on the throat plate of your sewing machine to allow for the proper seam allowances. Since you will determine your seam line by following the outside edge of the fabric rather than by following a line you have traced onto the fabric it is not possible to adjust for a mistake in cutting while you are sewing.

Of course, we can't hope to be as precise as the Egyptians when they built the Great Pyramid at Giza, which had sides 756 feet long and was constructed with an error of only $\frac{2}{3}$ of an inch, but we can try!

With this need for precision in mind, we have reproduced the outlines for most of the templates needed to make any quilt illustrated in this book. All you have to do to make an accurate template pattern is to trace the template outline exactly from the page.

Some of the template outlines are too large to fit on the pages in this book. If a design requires one of the templates which could not be included, this fact is noted in the page notes for that design in the *50 Traditional Patchwork Designs* chapter. Instructions for making these templates begin on page 206.

Using the template codes

To simplify the charts in this book, we have assigned a template code to each different shape and size template. These codes are simple to use and follow in a logical sequence. The first letter of the code indicates its shape: S stands for square, R for rectangle, T for triangle, and P for parallelogram. The number following the letter indicates the template size: the smaller the number, the smaller the template.

It is important to note that the seam allowance of $\frac{3}{8}''$ is included in the templates on pages 208–214. However, on the Template Code Reference Chart, the seam allowance is not included—the measurements are given for the templates *after* they are pieced together in the quilt top. (We have done this because, should you create your own design and want to check whether the necessary templates are available here, it will be much less confusing to check our chart listing for the *finished* size rather than the size plus seam allowance.)

Furthermore, the measurements on the Template Code Reference Chart include only two sides of each template. The dotted lines in Illustration 77 denote the sides given in the chart listing.

Illustration 77

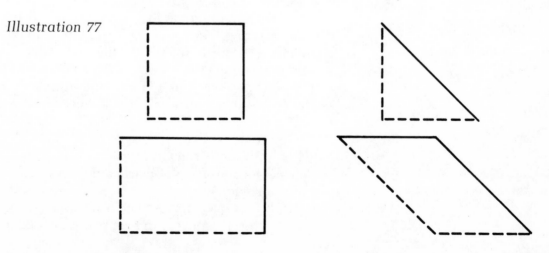

Template code reference chart

Because of the limitations of the page size in this book, not all of the templates which have been assigned codes are reproduced here. For your easy reference, the templates printed in black are reproduced and the ones printed in blue are not. (Instructions on how to draw the templates which are not provided follow on page 206.)

SQUARE

S1 = 2″ x 2″	S4 = 4″ x 4″	S7 = 8″ x 8″
S2 = 2½″ x 2½″	S5 = 5″ x 5″	S8 = 10″ x 10″
S3 = 3″ x 3″	S6 = 6″ x 6″	

RECTANGLE

R1 = 2″ x 4″	R4 = 4″ x 8″	R7 = 5″ x 15″
R2 = 2½″ x 5″	R5 = 4″ x 12″	R8 = 6″ x 18″
R3 = 3″ x 6″	R6 = 5″ x 10″	

PARALLELOGRAM

P1 = 3″ x 4½″	P2 = 4″ x 5⅝″	P3 = 5″ x 7$\frac{1}{16}$″

TRIANGLE

T1 = 2″ x 2″	T7 = 4¼″ x 4¼″	T12 = 8″ x 8″
T2 = 2½″ x 2½″	T8 = 5″ x 5″	T13 = 10″ x 10″
T3 = 2¾″ x 2¾″	T9 = 5⅝″ x 5⅝″	T14 = 12″ x 12″
T4 = 3″ x 3″	T10 = 6″ x 6″	T15 = 15″ x 15″
T5 = 3½″ x 3½″	T11 = 7$\frac{1}{16}$″ x 7$\frac{1}{16}$″	T16 = 18″ x 18″
T6 = 4″ x 4″		

Making templates

To make a template, you will need the following materials:

■ *paper for tracing the template from the book* If you need a template that is not reproduced in the book, go to page 206 for directions on how to make a template "from scratch."

■ *a stiff material to use as the base of the template* Stiff cardboard works well until the corners become rounded from repeated tracing. Therefore, if you use cardboard as the template base and are going to trace hundreds of patches from this template, it is a good idea to make several copies of the template. The flat plastic lids from coffee cans are excellent because the corners do not wear down, but you are limited to some extent by the size of the lid! Stiff fine-grain sandpaper is also good, especially since the sandpaper surface grips the fabric while tracing.

■ *white glue or rubber cement*
■ *sharp scissors*
■ *sharpened pencil or fine marking pen*

The template chart given for each design in the *50 Traditional Patchwork Designs* chapter indicates the total number of templates you must cut. If you are using an alternate design or an original design, you will determine this number by using the Designer's Worksheet. In either case, have the list of all required templates beside you for easy reference as you make your templates. That way, you will be sure to make all of the templates you need at one time.

Trace the outline of the template onto tracing paper. Use a sharpened pencil or fine marking pen so that your lines will not be too thick. The template outlines in the book are perfect and your template should match the outline provided.

Some templates are larger than the pages of this book and thus the total template outline could not be shown. However, for some of these templates, a portion of the template outline is provided, with directions to fold the tracing paper. Where a fold is indicated by a dotted line on one side of the template outline, simply fold your tracing paper in half, place the fold on the dotted line, and cut along the solid lines of the outline. When you unfold the template pattern it will be the correct size.

Two fold lines are indicated on the template outline for Template S8. To cut this template, fold your tracing paper in quarters, place the two folds on the two dotted lines of the outline, and cut along the two solid lines.

Next, glue the tracing paper on the stiff material you are using for the base of the template. Then, cut both the tracing paper and the stiff material along the outline of the template, making sure that the edges are smooth.

Mark each template pattern with the Template Code. That way, as you cut your fabric you can easily check that you are cutting the right template in the right color. It is also a good idea to indicate the number of pieces you need to cut from each color fabric on the template.

Determining the templates needed for any non-traditional design

If you are using one of the traditional designs illustrated in this book, the size and shape of the templates needed for constructing that block are listed on the chart accompanying the design. If you are using one of the alternate designs or a completely new design, you will have to determine for yourself

Illustration 78
Cat's Cradle

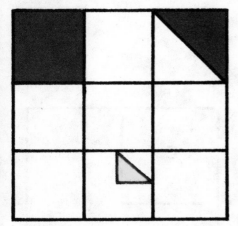

Illustration 79

what size templates you need. When you develop your own designs, you may want to combine two templates from a traditional design to form a larger shape. You will want to use only one template for this shape. The method outlined below will allow you to determine whether the outline for that template is provided.

To help you identify the templates, we have drawn each template in relation to an entire block. The possible block sizes are listed horizontally across the top of each chart: 12″, 15″, or 18″ for three-patch designs, and 12″, 16″, and 20″ for four-patch designs.

The letters down the left side of each chart correspond to the letters used to identify each template size in the illustration.

To determine the templates needed for your design, draw your design and the outline of each template in the blocks provided. Trace the template outlines onto tracing paper and place the tracing paper over the illustrations, matching the template outlines. Then use the chart below each illustration to determine the Template Code.

To illustrate this method, we will use **Cat's Cradle** in a 15″ block. First, the complete design is shown in the three-patch block outline (*Illustration 78*). Then each different size and shape template is shown once in the outline block (*Illustration 79*). In this design, there are three different shapes and sizes of templates—two triangles and one square. By comparing these template shapes against our reference chart, we find that the Template Codes are T8, T2, and S5.

You can quickly determine the templates required for any design in this book by first drawing the design in the appropriate box below and outlining the different template shapes. Then, trace the template outlines onto tracing paper. Place the tracing paper over the reference charts to match the template outlines.

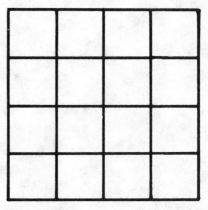

Rectangles

3-patch

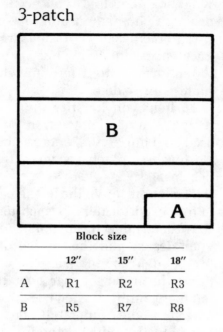

Block size			
	12″	15″	18″
A	R1	R2	R3
B	R5	R7	R8

4-patch

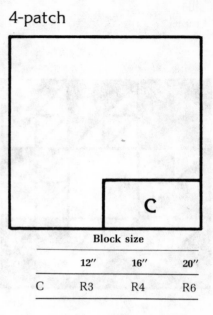

Block size			
	12″	16″	20″
C	R3	R4	R6

Squares

3-patch

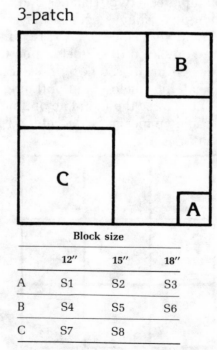

Block size			
	12″	15″	18″
A	S1	S2	S3
B	S4	S5	S6
C	S7	S8	

4-patch

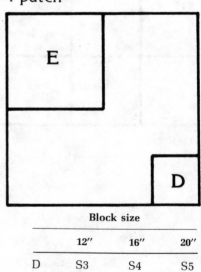

Block size			
	12″	16″	20″
D	S3	S4	S5
E	S6	S7	S8

Triangles

3-patch

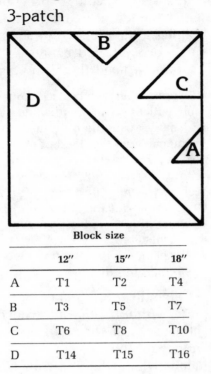

Block size			
	12″	15″	18″
A	T1	T2	T4
B	T3	T5	T7
C	T6	T8	T10
D	T14	T15	T16

4-patch

Block size			
	12″	16″	20″
E	T4	T6	T8
F	T7	T9	T11
G	T10	T12	T13

Parallelograms

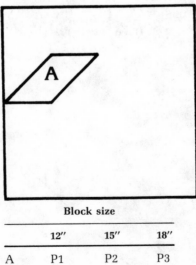

Block size			
	12″	15″	18″
A	P1	P2	P3

Making your own template outlines

If the size of your chosen block design requires templates which could not be included in this book, the instructions for making a template from scratch, while a little more complicated, are outlined below.

You will need the following materials:

- *graph paper* The best kind of graph paper has eight squares to the inch, with every inch indicated by a heavy line as in Illustration 80. It is usually available only in drafting supply stores.
If you can't get this kind of graph paper, any kind will do so long as any number of the squares into which it is ruled will fit precisely within a square inch. If it doesn't provide the heavy lines indicating inches, you may find it helpful to draw them in yourself.
- *stiff material for the base of the template*
- *white glue or rubber cement*
- *sharp scissors*
- *sharpened pencil or fine marking pen*
- *cellophane tape*

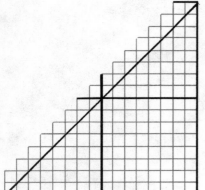

Illustration 80

Using the graph paper, outline the dimensions of your template *without* seam allowances. You might have to tape together several sheets of graph paper to obtain a piece large enough for the largest templates. Use the heavy lines indicating inches when drawing your template (*Illustration 81*).

If you use graph paper ruled eight squares to the inch, your seam allowance lines will be a cinch, since each square equals ⅛″. Simply count three of these squares and draw your seam allowance line. If you don't have this kind of graph paper, measure ⅜″ from the outline of your template and draw the seam allowance lines (*Illustration 82*).

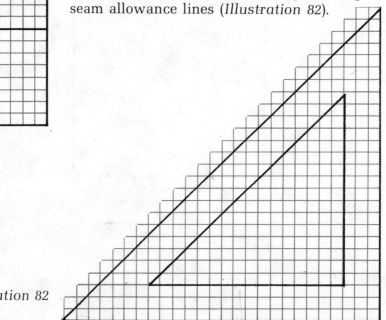

Illustration 81

Illustration 82

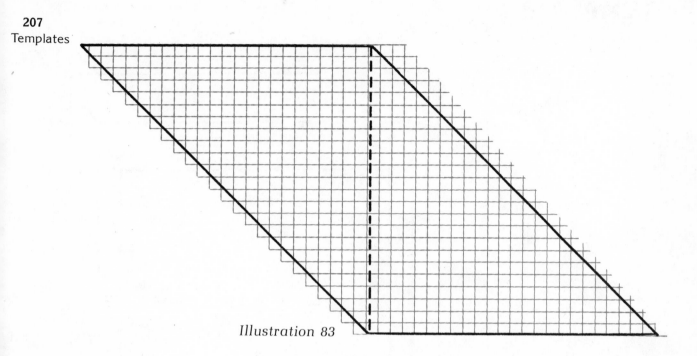

Illustration 83

To complete your template pattern, follow the steps outlined above (in the section on Making Templates) on how to glue the graph paper on the stiffener. Then, cut out your template using the seam allowance lines as your guide.

Drawing squares, triangles, and rectangles is very easy, but we have one final hint for parallelograms. Parallelograms are really two right triangles of equal dimensions connected on one side. If you measure the base of your parallelogram (the base measurement in template P1 is 3″, in P2 is 4″, and in P3 is 5″) and draw it on your graph paper, then measure the same number of inches at right angles to your base line, the top of your parallelogram begins at that point and also equals the measurement of the base. Connecting the top and bottom lines will complete the outline (*Illustration 83*).

RECTANGLE TEMPLATES

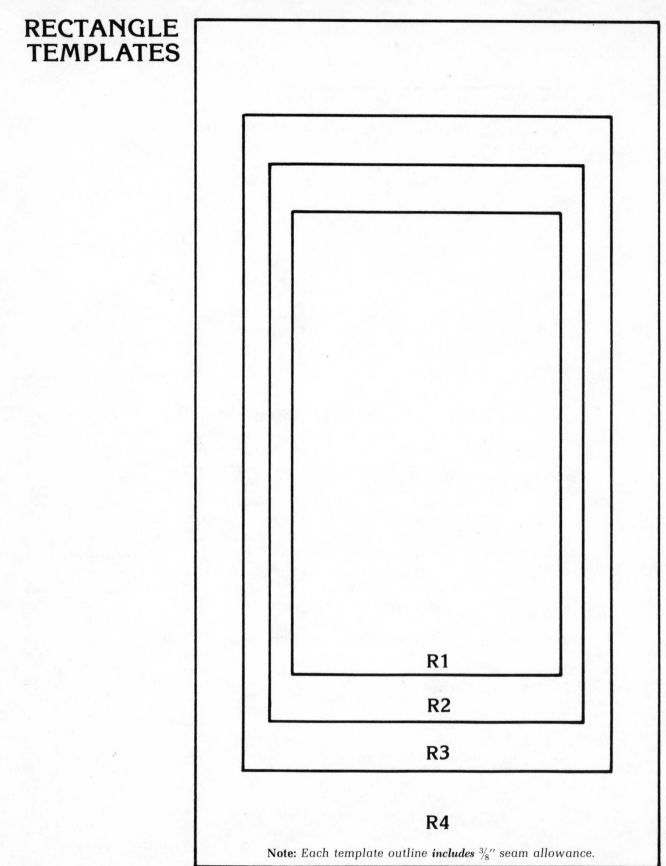

R1

R2

R3

R4

Note: *Each template outline **includes** $\frac{3}{8}''$ seam allowance.*

RECTANGLE
TEMPLATES

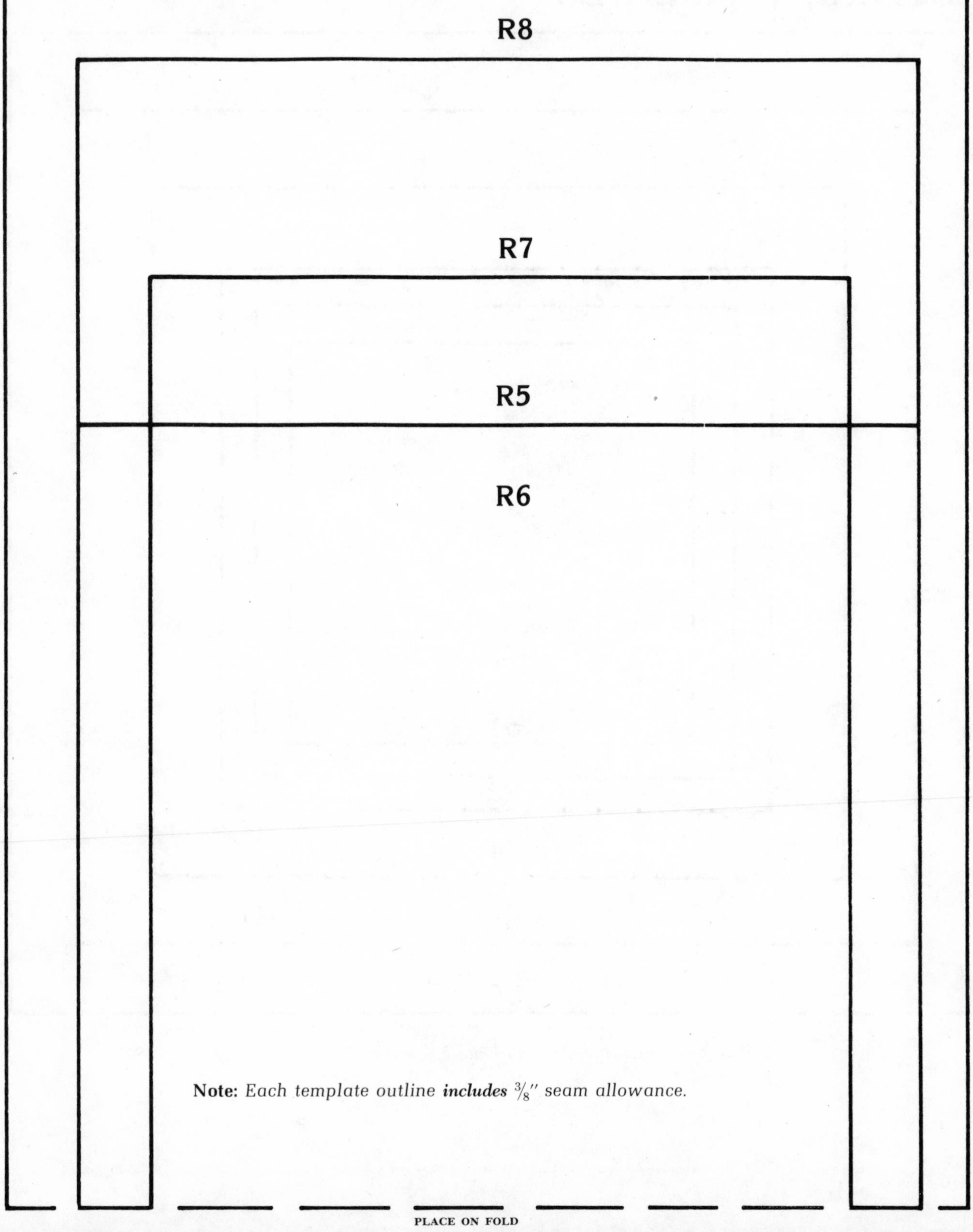

R8

R7

R5

R6

Note: Each template outline *includes* ⅜″ seam allowance.

SQUARE TEMPLATES

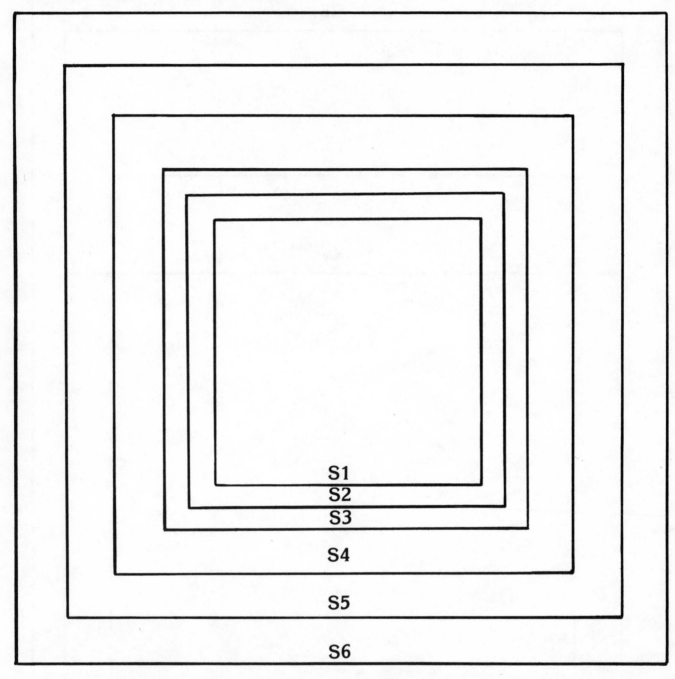

S1
S2
S3
S4
S5
S6

Note: *Each template outline **includes** ³⁄₈″ seam allowance.*

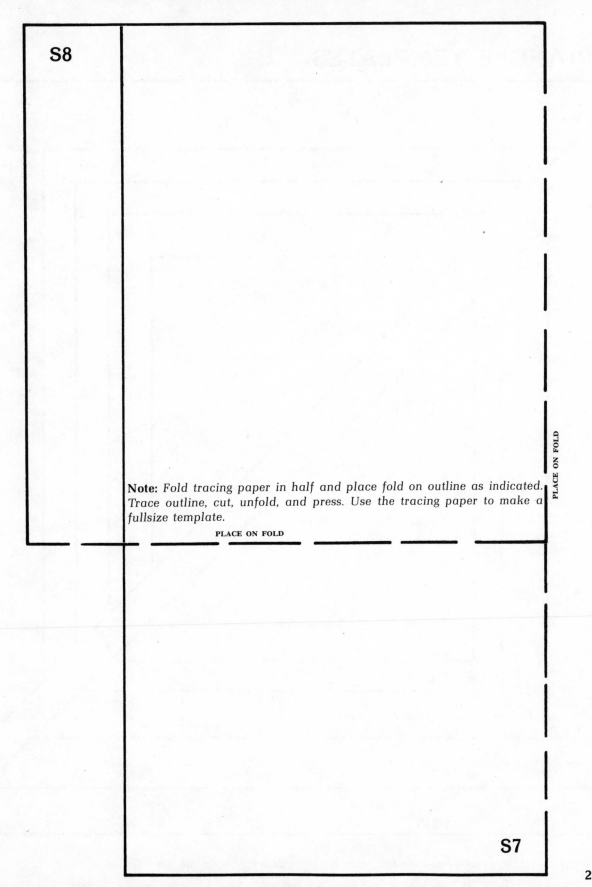

S8

Note: Fold tracing paper in half and place fold on outline as indicated. Trace outline, cut, unfold, and press. Use the tracing paper to make a fullsize template.

PLACE ON FOLD

PLACE ON FOLD

S7

Note: Each template outline *includes* ⅜″ seam allowance.

TRIANGLE TEMPLATES

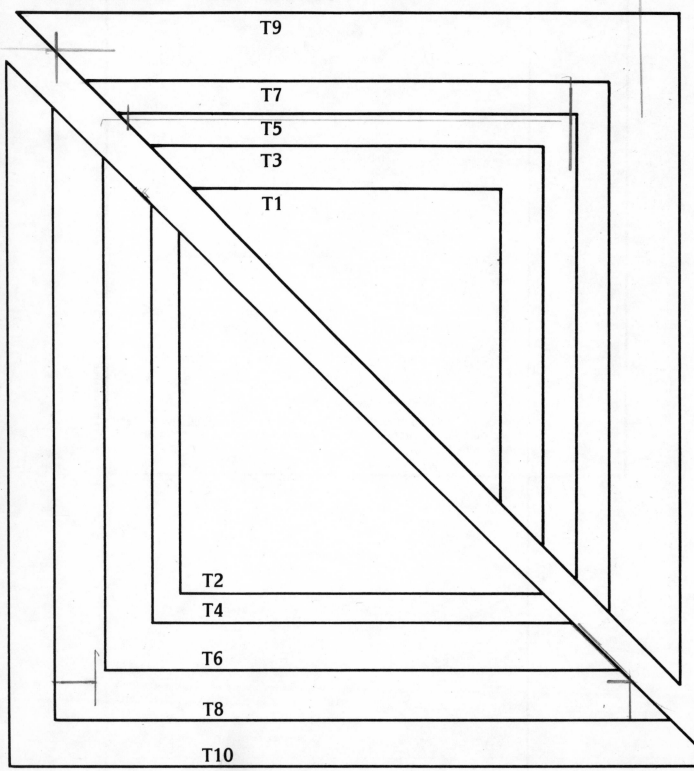

T9

T7

T5

T3

T1

T2

T4

T6

T8

T10

Note: *Each template outline **includes** ³⁄₈″ seam allowance.*

TRIANGLE TEMPLATES

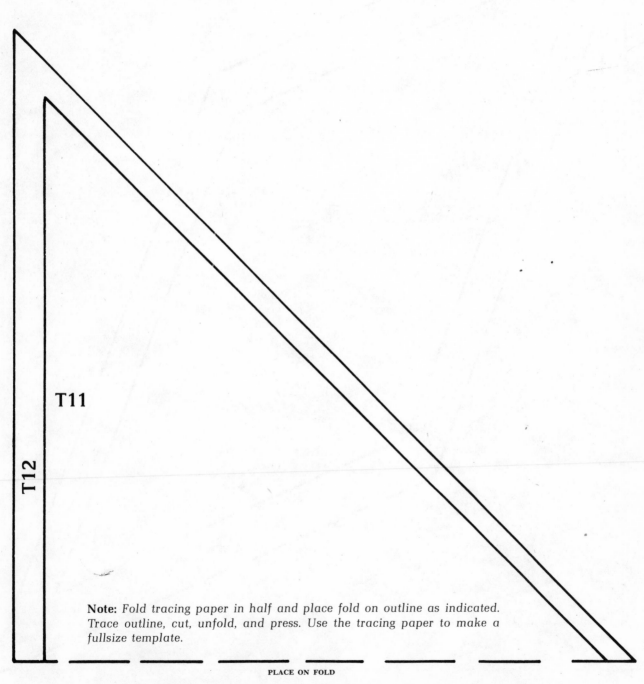

T11

T12

Note: *Fold tracing paper in half and place fold on outline as indicated. Trace outline, cut, unfold, and press. Use the tracing paper to make a fullsize template.*

PLACE ON FOLD

Note: *Each template outline **includes** ³⁄₈″ seam allowance.*

PARALLELOGRAM TEMPLATES

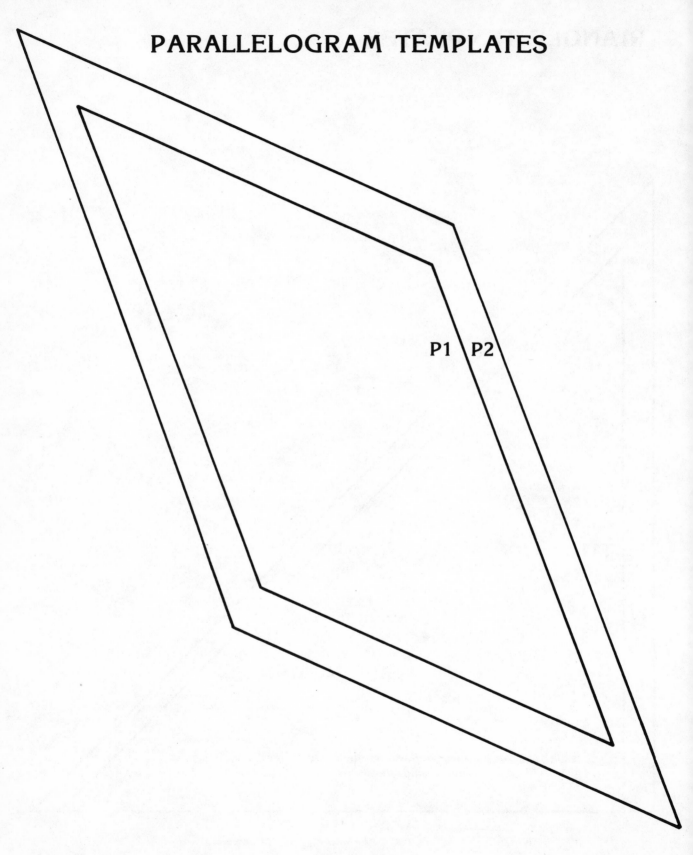

P1 P2

9
Yardage Charts

Using the charts on the following pages, you can easily and quickly determine how many yards of fabric will be needed for each template in your quilt. The *Yardage Charts* are organized according to the shape and size of the template. For example, all of the rectangles are grouped on one chart, beginning with the smallest at the left of the chart.

All you have to do to determine the yardage required is to locate the *Template Code,* read vertically until you come to the number of templates for the quilt you are planning, then follow that line to the left of the chart where the number of yards of fabric required to make that number of templates is listed.

Let's take an example. On the chart provided for the traditional design **Old Maid's Puzzle** in the *50 Traditional Patchwork Designs* chapter, we have indicated in blue the number of templates required for a king-size quilt made from 16″ blocks.

Templates	Color	Code	Number of pieces needed for quilt			
			Twin	Full	Queen	King
△	blue	T6	350	420	420	490
□	blue	S4	140	168	168	196
△	red	T6	210	252	252	294
△	red	T12	70	84	84	98
		Totals	**770**	**924**	**924**	**1,078**

As the chart above indicates, 98 pieces cut in the shape of template T12 will be needed for the construction of this quilt top. Using the sample Yardage Chart, you can quickly determine the yardage required for these templates: simply read down column T12 until you reach the line in which the number given equals or exceeds 98. Here, that number is 102. Now read left across the chart to the yardage column and you learn that $4\frac{3}{4}$ yards of 36" fabric will be needed.

Note that the Yardage Charts begin with $\frac{1}{4}$ yard and increase at intervals of $\frac{1}{4}$ yard up to 5 yards. If the number of templates you need will require more than 5 yards of fabric, first note the number that can be cut from 5 yards. Then subtract that number from the total number of templates needed. Read back down the chart until you reach that remaining number of templates and determine the required yardage. This additional yardage added to the original 5 yards will equal the total amount of fabric you will need.

For example, for template code T6, to be done in blue, we need 490 templates. However, only 360 templates are available from 5 yards of fabric. So we note this amount, subtract it from the total (490) and learn that we need an additional 130 templates. Going back to the yardage chart, we find that 130 templates will require an additional 2 yards of fabric. This 2 yards added to the original 5 yards gives us a total of 7 yards necessary to make 490 templates of code T6.

Almost all cotton fabrics come in 36" or 45" widths. Therefore, there are separate charts indicating how many templates can be cut from fabric in either width. Since you will not know what width fabric you will use until you have actually been to the fabric store, we suggest that you determine the yardage necessary for each template from *both* 36" and 45" wide material. If you do, you will be prepared to buy all the fabric you need, but not more than you need.

We have allowed $\frac{1}{4}$" between each template on the sides and between the rows. We have done this so that each template is separately traced and cut. You could squeeze a few more

Yardage Chart for 36" wide fabric

Yards	Template Codes							
	T9	T10	T11	T12	T13	T14	T15	T16
1/4	8	8	8	—	—	—	—	—
1/2	16	16	16	6	6	4	4	—
3/4	24	24	24	12	12	4	4	2
1	32	32	32	18	18	8	8	2
1 1/4	40	40	40	24	18	12	8	4
1 1/2	48	48	48	30	24	12	12	4
1 3/4	64	56	56	36	30	16	12	6
2	72	72	64	42	36	20	16	6
2 1/4	80	80	72	48	36	20	16	8
2 1/2	88	88	80	54	42	24	20	8
2 3/4	96	96	88	54	48	28	20	8
3	104	104	96	60	54	28	24	10
3 1/4	120	112	104	66	54	32	24	10
3 1/2	128	120	112	72	60	36	28	12
3 3/4	136	128	120	78	66	36	28	12
4	144	144	128	84	72	40	32	14
4 1/4	152	152	136	90	72	40	36	14
4 1/2	160	160	144	96	78	44	36	16
4 3/4	176	168	152	102	84	48	40	16
5	184	176	160	108	90	48	40	18

templates out of some yardages if you placed the templates right next to each other when tracing. However, we find that tracing each template separately and leaving some space between them helps maintain the precision in cutting that is essential.

Special placement of rectangles

When tracing the rectangular templates, sometimes you are able to cut more pieces by placing the shorter side parallel to the selvage and sometimes by placing the longer side parallel to the selvage. You will note that on the *Yardage Charts* for rectangular templates, some of the numbers are printed in black and some are printed in blue. These colors denote the way to trace the templates to maximize the fabric usage: when printed in black, place the template so that the shorter side is parallel to the selvage; when printed in blue, place the longer side of the template parallel to the selvage.

Determining yardage requirements for borders

After you have determined the border size you want, following the instructions on page 30, follow these two steps to determine the amount of fabric you will need:

1 Write down the number and size of the strips you need.

2 side strips measuring _____ x _____ (The length of each side
width   length
piece should equal the length of the finished quilt plus $\frac{3}{4}''$ for the seam allowances on all sides and ends.)

1 bottom strip measuring _____ x _____ (The length of the
width   length
bottom piece should equal the width of the finished quilt, minus the combined widths of the side borders, plus $\frac{3}{4}''$ for the seam allowances.)

Let's take an example. The border requirements for a queen-size quilt using a 16″ block are 4″ on each side and 5″ on the bottom. We know that the finished quilt should measure 104″ wide and 117″ long. Using this information, we can fill in the number and size of each strip needed:

2 side strips measuring _____ x _____
width   length

1 bottom strip measuring _____ x _____
width   length

2 The next step is to determine how much fabric you need to cut out these strips. Take the longest strip measurement and divide by 36″, the number of inches in one yard. This figure will tell you how many yards of fabric to buy for your border.
Example: In our queen-size quilt, the longest strip measures 117″. Adding $\frac{3}{4}''$ for seam allowances, and dividing by 36″, we find that we need $3\frac{3}{8}$ yards of fabric.
Note: If you are using very wide borders and the combined width of the three strips is greater than the width of the fabric you will be using, you must add additional yardage.

Determining yardage requirements for lining

The following chart shows the amount of fabric required to line a standard-size bedspread:

Width of fabric	Twin	Full	Queen	King
36″	$9\frac{1}{3}$ yds.	$9\frac{1}{3}$ yds.	$9\frac{3}{4}$ yds.	$13\frac{1}{2}$ yds
45″	5 yds.	$9\frac{3}{4}$ yds.	$9\frac{3}{4}$ yds.	$10\frac{1}{4}$ yds.

If you are making a twin- or full-size quilt, you may want to use a sheet for the lining. Sheeting is inexpensive, the material is a good weight, and best of all there will be no seams on the underside.

If you are using an adjusted quilt size, rather than a standard size, you can determine the amount of material required for the lining by following these steps:

1 Begin by noting the total size of your quilt in the spaces below:

Quilt width _____ *inches*   Quilt length _____ *inches*

2 To determine how many strips you need to cover the width of your quilt, divide the quilt width by the width of your fabric minus one inch for the seam allowances.

$$\frac{\text{Quilt width}}{\text{Width of fabric less } 1''} = \text{Number of strips needed for width}$$

If your answer contains a fraction (for example, 3.5) round *up* to the nearest whole number (for example, 3.5 becomes 4)

3 Multiply the number of strips needed for the width by the number of inches in your quilt length (as noted in step 1 above)

Number of strips _____ × Number of inches in length _____

= _____ Total number of inches of fabric

4 Divide the total number of inches needed for the length of your quilt by 37 to determine the number of yards (including seam allowances) you need for the quilt lining.

Total number of inches _____ ÷ 37

= _____ Total number of yards needed

Round your answer up to the nearest ¼ yard.

Squares

Yardage Chart for 36″ wide fabric

Yards	Template Codes							
	S1	S2	S3	S4	S5	S6	S7	S8
$\frac{1}{4}$	36	20	18	7	6	5	4	—
$\frac{1}{2}$	72	50	36	21	18	10	8	3
$\frac{3}{4}$	108	70	54	35	24	15	12	6
1	144	100	81	49	36	25	16	9
$1\frac{1}{4}$	180	120	99	63	42	30	20	12
$1\frac{1}{2}$	216	150	117	70	54	35	24	12
$1\frac{3}{4}$	252	180	135	84	60	45	28	15
2	288	200	162	98	72	50	32	18
$2\frac{1}{4}$	324	230	180	112	78	55	36	21
$2\frac{1}{2}$	360	250	198	126	90	60	40	24
$2\frac{3}{4}$	396	280	216	133	96	70	44	27
3	432	300	243	147	108	75	48	27
$3\frac{1}{4}$	468	330	261	161	114	80	52	30
$3\frac{1}{2}$	504	360	279	175	126	90	56	33
$3\frac{3}{4}$	540	380	297	189	132	95	60	36
4	576	410	324	196	144	100	64	39
$4\frac{1}{4}$	612	430	342	210	150	105	68	39
$4\frac{1}{2}$	648	460	360	224	162	115	72	42
$4\frac{3}{4}$	684	480	378	238	168	120	76	45
5	720	510	405	252	180	125	80	48

Yardage Chart for 45″ wide fabric

Yards	Template Codes							
	S1	S2	S3	S4	S5	S6	S7	S8
$\frac{1}{4}$	45	24	22	9	7	6	5	—
$\frac{1}{2}$	90	48	44	27	21	12	10	4
$\frac{3}{4}$	135	84	66	45	28	18	15	8
1	180	108	99	63	42	30	20	12
$1\frac{1}{4}$	225	144	121	81	49	36	25	16
$1\frac{1}{2}$	270	168	143	90	63	42	30	16
$1\frac{3}{4}$	315	192	165	108	70	54	35	20
2	360	228	198	126	84	60	40	24
$2\frac{1}{4}$	405	252	220	144	91	66	45	28
$2\frac{1}{2}$	450	288	242	162	105	72	50	32
$2\frac{3}{4}$	495	312	264	171	112	84	55	36
3	540	336	297	189	126	90	60	36
$3\frac{1}{4}$	585	372	319	207	133	96	65	40
$3\frac{1}{2}$	630	396	341	225	147	108	70	44
$3\frac{3}{4}$	675	432	363	243	154	114	75	48
4	720	456	396	252	168	120	80	52
$4\frac{1}{4}$	765	480	418	270	175	126	85	52
$4\frac{1}{2}$	810	516	440	288	189	138	90	56
$4\frac{3}{4}$	855	540	462	306	196	144	95	60
5	900	576	495	324	210	150	100	64

Rectangles

Yardage Chart for 36″ wide fabric

Yards	R1	R2	R3	R4	R5	R6	R7	R8
1/4	21	12	10	7	2	3	2	1
1/2	42	30	20	14	7	9	6	2
3/4	63	42	30	21	14	12	8	5
1	84	60	45	28	14	18	12	5
1 1/4	108	72	55	36	21	24	14	10
1 1/2	126	90	65	42	28	27	18	10
1 3/4	147	108	81	49	28	30	20	15
2	168	120	90	56	35	36	24	15
2 1/4	192	138	100	64	42	42	30	20
2 1/2	216	150	110	72	42	48	30	20
2 3/4	231	168	126	77	49	54	36	25
3	252	180	135	84	56	54	36	25
3 1/4	276	198	145	92	63	60	42	30
3 1/2	300	216	162	100	63	66	42	30
3 3/4	324	228	171	108	70	72	48	35
4	336	246	180	112	77	78	54	35
4 1/4	360	258	190	120	77	78	54	40
4 1/2	384	276	207	128	84	84	60	40
4 3/4	408	288	216	136	91	90	60	45
5	432	306	225	144	91	96	66	45

Yardage Chart for 45″ wide fabric

Yards	R1	R2	R3	R4	R5	R6	R7	R8
1/4	27	18	12	9	3	4	2	2
1/2	54	45	24	18	9	12	7	4
3/4	81	63	36	27	18	16	8	6
1	108	90	55	36	21	24	14	10
1 1/4	135	108	66	45	27	28	14	12
1 1/2	162	135	78	54	36	36	21	14
1 3/4	189	162	99	63	36	40	21	18
2	216	180	110	72	45	48	28	20
2 1/4	243	207	121	81	54	52	35	24
2 1/2	270	225	132	90	54	60	35	24
2 3/4	295	252	154	99	63	64	42	30
3	324	270	165	108	72	72	42	30
3 1/4	351	297	176	117	81	76	49	36
3 1/2	378	324	198	126	81	84	49	36
3 3/4	405	342	209	135	90	88	56	42
4	432	369	221	144	99	96	63	42
4 1/4	459	387	231	153	99	100	63	48
4 1/2	486	414	253	162	108	108	60	48
4 3/4	513	432	264	171	117	112	60	54
5	540	459	275	180	117	120	66	54

Special Note: To obtain the number of templates stated in this chart and to eliminate wastage or shortage, the numbers in black indicate that the shortest side of the template is placed parallel to the selvage and the numbers printed in blue indicate that the longest side is placed parallel to the selvage.

Triangles

Yardage Chart for 36″ wide fabric

Yards	Template Codes							
	T1	T2	T3	T4	T5	T6	T7	T8
¼	36	32	14	14	12	12	10	10
½	72	64	42	42	36	36	20	20
¾	108	96	70	70	48	48	40	30
1	162	128	98	98	72	72	50	50
1¼	198	160	126	126	96	84	70	60
1½	234	192	154	140	108	108	80	70
1¾	270	224	182	168	132	120	100	90
2	324	256	210	196	156	144	110	100
2¼	360	288	238	224	168	156	120	110
2½	396	320	252	252	192	180	140	120
2¾	432	352	280	266	216	192	150	140
3	486	384	308	294	228	216	170	150
3¼	522	416	336	322	252	228	180	160
3½	558	448	364	350	264	252	200	180
3¾	594	480	392	378	288	264	210	190
4	648	512	420	392	312	288	230	200
4¼	684	544	448	420	324	300	240	210
4½	720	576	476	448	348	324	250	230
4¾	756	608	504	476	372	336	270	240
5	810	640	518	504	384	360	280	250

Yardage Chart for 45″ wide fabric

Yards	Template Codes							
	T1	T2	T3	T4	T5	T6	T7	T8
¼	44	40	18	18	16	14	14	12
½	88	80	54	54	48	42	28	24
¾	132	120	90	90	64	56	56	36
1	198	160	126	126	96	84	70	60
1¼	242	200	162	162	128	98	98	72
1½	286	240	198	180	144	126	112	84
1¾	330	280	234	216	176	140	140	108
2	396	320	270	252	208	168	154	120
2¼	440	360	306	288	224	182	168	132
2½	484	400	324	324	256	210	196	144
2¾	528	440	360	342	288	224	210	168
3	594	480	396	378	304	252	238	180
3¼	638	520	432	414	336	266	252	192
3½	682	560	468	450	352	294	280	216
3¾	726	600	504	486	384	308	294	228
4	792	640	540	504	416	336	322	240
4¼	836	680	576	540	432	350	336	252
4½	880	720	612	576	464	378	350	276
4¾	924	760	648	612	496	392	378	288
5	990	800	666	648	512	420	392	300

Yardage Chart for 36″ wide fabric

Yards	Template Codes							
	T9	T10	T11	T12	T13	T14	T15	T16
$\frac{1}{4}$	8	8	8	—	—	—	—	—
$\frac{1}{2}$	16	16	16	6	6	4	4	—
$\frac{3}{4}$	24	24	24	12	12	4	4	2
1	32	32	32	18	18	8	8	2
$1\frac{1}{4}$	40	40	40	24	18	12	8	4
$1\frac{1}{2}$	48	48	48	30	24	12	12	4
$1\frac{3}{4}$	64	56	56	36	30	16	12	6
2	72	72	64	42	36	20	16	6
$2\frac{1}{4}$	80	80	72	48	36	20	16	8
$2\frac{1}{2}$	88	88	80	54	42	24	20	8
$2\frac{3}{4}$	96	96	88	54	48	28	20	8
3	104	104	96	60	54	28	24	10
$3\frac{1}{4}$	120	112	104	66	54	32	24	10
$3\frac{1}{2}$	128	120	112	72	60	36	28	12
$3\frac{3}{4}$	136	128	120	78	66	36	28	12
4	144	144	128	84	72	40	32	14
$4\frac{1}{4}$	152	152	136	90	72	40	36	14
$4\frac{1}{2}$	160	160	144	96	78	44	36	16
$4\frac{3}{4}$	176	168	152	102	84	48	40	16
5	184	176	160	108	90	48	40	18

Yardage Chart for 45″ wide fabric

Yards	Template Codes							
	T9	T10	T11	T12	T13	T14	T15	T16
$\frac{1}{4}$	10	10	10	—	—	—	—	—
$\frac{1}{2}$	20	20	20	8	6	6	4	—
$\frac{3}{4}$	30	30	30	16	12	6	4	4
1	40	40	40	24	18	12	8	4
$1\frac{1}{4}$	50	50	50	32	18	18	8	8
$1\frac{1}{2}$	60	60	60	40	24	18	12	8
$1\frac{3}{4}$	80	70	70	48	30	24	12	12
2	90	90	80	56	36	30	16	12
$2\frac{1}{4}$	100	100	90	64	36	30	16	16
$2\frac{1}{2}$	110	110	100	72	42	36	20	16
$2\frac{3}{4}$	120	120	110	72	48	42	20	16
3	130	130	120	80	54	42	24	20
$3\frac{1}{4}$	150	140	130	88	54	48	24	20
$3\frac{1}{2}$	160	150	140	96	60	54	28	24
$3\frac{3}{4}$	170	160	150	104	66	54	28	24
4	180	180	160	112	72	60	32	28
$4\frac{1}{4}$	190	190	170	120	72	60	36	28
$4\frac{1}{2}$	200	200	180	128	78	66	36	32
$4\frac{3}{4}$	220	210	190	136	84	72	40	32
5	230	220	200	144	90	72	40	36

Parallelograms

Yardage Chart for 36″ wide fabric

Yards	Template Codes		
	P1	P2	P3
$\frac{1}{4}$	10	6	3
$\frac{1}{2}$	25	12	9
$\frac{3}{4}$	35	18	15
1	50	24	21
$1\frac{1}{4}$	60	30	27
$1\frac{1}{2}$	75	36	30
$1\frac{3}{4}$	90	42	36
2	100	48	42
$2\frac{1}{4}$	115	54	48
$2\frac{1}{2}$	125	60	54
$2\frac{3}{4}$	140	66	57
3	150	72	63
$3\frac{1}{4}$	165	78	69
$3\frac{1}{2}$	180	84	75
$3\frac{3}{4}$	190	90	81
4	205	96	84
$4\frac{1}{4}$	215	102	90
$4\frac{1}{2}$	230	108	96
$4\frac{3}{4}$	240	114	102
5	255	120	108

Yardage Chart for 45″ wide fabric

Yards	Template Codes		
	P1	P2	P3
$\frac{1}{4}$	12	10	4
$\frac{1}{2}$	30	20	12
$\frac{3}{4}$	42	30	20
1	60	40	24
$1\frac{1}{4}$	72	50	32
$1\frac{1}{2}$	90	60	40
$1\frac{3}{4}$	108	70	48
2	120	80	56
$2\frac{1}{4}$	138	90	64
$2\frac{1}{2}$	150	100	72
$2\frac{3}{4}$	168	110	76
3	180	120	84
$3\frac{1}{4}$	198	130	92
$3\frac{1}{2}$	216	140	100
$3\frac{3}{4}$	228	150	108
4	246	160	112
$4\frac{1}{4}$	258	170	120
$4\frac{1}{2}$	276	180	128
$4\frac{3}{4}$	288	190	136
5	306	200	144